MW01699618

With Faith Like Hers Bible Study Series

I am Eve

Carol Peterson

Honor Bound Books

HBB

Honor Bound Books

Typeset in 12/16/18pt Cambria; cover and title fonts 36 pt Lucinda Handwriting; logo 12 pt Lucinda Calligraphy. Used with permission from Microsoft. Cover logo font 20 pt Viner Hand ITC, used with permission from Adobe. Cover background and graphics used with permission from Adobe.

ISBN 13: 978-0692024348
ISBN 10: 0692024344

Dedication

This book is dedicated, with gratitude to my family and friends who have encouraged the writing of this series, especially to Jim and Nicole for their serious attention to detail and theology. It is also dedicated to the men and women whose lives are recorded in Scripture so that we, who seek to follow God's ways, can understand that He loves us, even though...

CONTENTS

Preface

It is human nature to explore who we are. It is part of the spiritual journey we take as Christians to explore who we are *in Christ* and seek to understand who God wants us to become. This women's Bible study series focuses on understanding ourselves as Christian women.

Scripture gives us examples of people who lived by faith. They were people just like us—with flaws and foibles; triumphs and turmoil. But they lived a victorious life because they lived in the light of God's love. Outward things have changed since biblical times, but people are basically the same. When we look at the lives of women in Scripture, we glimpse how God saw them. When we learn the lessons they learned, God can show us how He still sees His women today. We can say, "I am like her; I have her faith; I can survive her circumstances. I am she."

That is the basis of the *With Faith Like Hers* series. Each book takes the reader through 28 days of meditative Bible study. We look at a woman in Scripture and see how God—through His Word—viewed her and how He might view our lives in a similar manner. This is Eve's story. But it is also ours—when we have faith like hers.

Although this book is intended to be an individual daily study, it can also be used effectively as a group study. Simply divide each weekly discussion at the sections—discuss one section each week. Cover day 1 with the first week; cover day 28 with the final week. Some weeks will have fewer days than others, but none will require more than one reading per day. Additional study helps are available for this series online at www.HonorBoundBooks.com. I pray that you will be blessed in your study as you discover how God might see His women of faith.

A Note about Eve

Eve's story is unique. She didn't just believe in God. She knew God. Personally. She also, unfortunately, knew Satan personally.

Some people choose to look at the Adam and Eve account as allegory. They believe the writer of Genesis created a fictional couple to tell a story of how God might have begun creation. Others hold tight to the factualness of Scripture and believe the Genesis account is true to life in every detail.

Whether you believe Genesis was written as an exact representation of events or as a story intended to grow our faith, it has been included in our Holy Bible with truths for us to understand. Whether Eve was real or fictional, her life has been recorded in Scripture in a way that can help us learn something about our own character and circumstances today.

This study includes several chapters related to motherhood. I acknowledge that not all women have children, either by choice or circumstance. But we recognize the biological part women play in God's overall plan for humanity. I urge you therefore to remember, that even if you personally do not have children, there are lessons we can learn from the very fact that God created women with the ability to bear children.

So, come with me and let's find out what Eve might be telling us through the way her life has been recorded in Scripture for us today.

Day 1—Becoming Eve

I spent most of my life being annoyed by Eve! How could she listen to a snake? Who does that? Now the rest of us have to pay for her foolishness.

When God led me to write a series of Bible studies about women of the Bible, the usual came up—Ruth and Esther of course, having their very own books. And Mother Mary also felt like a natural.

But when God indicated that I should include Eve in this series, I wondered what God had in mind. Surely, as the woman whose actions caused the fall of human kind, God did not want me to write a book for women to see how we might be like *her*.

But in obedience and with an open mind, I sat down and read through Genesis looking for what Eve could teach me. In the reading, I heard God's whisper of love for her. I heard His justice for doing what was best for her. I heard His anguish at her disobedience. And I heard His whisper, justice and anguish for me, through Eve.

Because of the reading, my heart softened toward Eve. After all, she was just human. Like me. And as the first human woman, she was still trying to find her way in the great big world.

Like me. And making mistakes along the way. Like me. She was also trying to find her place in her relationship with the God of the universe. Like me.

Obviously God knew what He was doing (again) when leading me to write this study. Genesis isn't just a story about creation. It isn't just the sad retelling of sin coming into the world. It isn't just a gossipy tale, pointing fingers and casting blame at the man and woman responsible for our state of affairs today. Rather, Genesis recounts the beginning of a love story between our Holy God and His first children whom He loved with an everlasting love. Like He loves me.

And like He loves you.

As I've been writing this series *With Faith Like Hers,* God has pointed out one verse to focus on during the writing of each book. For this book, God gave me Genesis 1:27:

> *So God created mankind in his own image, in the image of God he created them; male and female he created them.*

Keeping this verse in mind helped me realize that, in spite of Eve's action that caused the downfall of mankind into sin, God created Eve in His own image, just as He created you and me. As a result, I could marvel at her circumstances.

To say Eve just had faith in God is inaccurate. Eve didn't struggle with the theoretical question of whether God existed. She didn't have to rely on theology or teaching by others who knew Scripture and church doctrine. She didn't need to attend services on Sunday or join a woman's Bible study class to know God. She didn't just have a spiritually-founded relationship with God. She literally could walk and talk with God in the Garden. She didn't just have faith; she had knowledge.

How well do we know God? What type of relationship do we have with the God of the universe? What kind of relationship *could* we have if our faith was more about knowing God than spouting doctrine? Or about understanding what is behind doctrine because it is the story of God's plan and His love for us?

For this first day, please start reading through Genesis chapters 1, 2 and 3. Those chapters will take us through the Fall—where Adam and Eve disobeyed God and as judgment, were forced from the Garden. The chapters are short, but filled with lessons. We'll take them one a day for the next 27 days.

This book is Eve's story. But it is also ours. As we study together, perhaps we'll find out how we are like Eve—if we have faith like hers.

For Thought and Discussion

- What has been your opinion of Eve to date? Does it include judgment, anger or annoyance?

- If you could literally walk in the Garden with Jesus today, what would be the first thing you would say or ask?

- In what area of your faith do you feel God leading you to become stronger? Are you willing to consider how Eve might teach you in that area of your faith?

PRAYER: Heavenly Father, thank you for our lives. Thank you for creating our lives as women, starting with your very first woman, Eve. Thank you for preserving her life in Scripture. Please open our minds and hearts to whatever lessons you want us to learn from your daughter, Eve. Amen.

I am God's Creation

Day 2—I am Made in God's Image

When I look at the world, sometimes I can't contain my giggles. I see a cactus or a duck and wonder what God was thinking when He created them. Even looking at us human beings is funny. Imagine life without eyebrows or toenails. Imagine knees that bend sideways or ears located under our armpits. Or having no armpits at all. God did such a perfect job when He created us. Our form is perfect because our form is also God's.

> *So God created mankind in his own image, in the image of God he created them; male and female he created them* (Genesis 1:27).

One of the basic beliefs of Christianity is that Jesus is one equal part of the Trinity: Father, Son and Holy Spirit. All three persons of the Trinity combine in a supernatural way as one God, triune in nature. God is one essence that never changes; but God also is three distinct and complete persons. Our human minds may not understand the complexity of the Trinity, but Scripture clearly refers to God in all three of these manners: as Father, as Son Jesus and as the Holy Spirit.

The appearance of God the Father is described in Scripture vaguely as "the glory of the Lord" (Acts 7:55), "brightness" (1 Timothy 6:16) or a cloud or pillar of fire (Exodus). Moses stood in God's presence but was shielded by the Father's hand and placed in a cleft in the rock so Moses would not be killed by the glory of God. Descriptions are vague because evidently mankind cannot handle seeing the Father's true appearance, except as "through a mirror dimly" (1 Corinthians 13:12). Jesus Himself told us that *"No one has seen the Father except the one who is from God; only he* (Jesus) *has seen the Father."* (John 6:46, explanation added).

We cannot see the Holy Spirit either. Scripture describes Him as hovering (Genesis 1:2; Acts 2:3) and being able to dwell in us (Acts 2:31; Romans 8:9). Since neither God the Father nor the Holy Spirit exist in human form, clearly mankind was not made in the image of either God the Father or God the Holy Spirit. The only one of the three persons to have human form we can see is Jesus.

When Jesus lived on earth 2,000 years ago, he took male form. The important point here is that he took *human* form. You and I—like Jesus—have a physical body that is similar in structure and purpose.

In addition to being born physically as a human on earth, Jesus was also "there in the beginning." It is Jesus who the Apostle John referred to as *logos*, "the spoken word," telling us it was Jesus who spoke creation into being.

> *In the beginning was the word* (Jesus) *and the word* (Jesus) *was with God and the word* (Jesus) was *God* (John 1:1, explanation added).

Jesus was there in the beginning of everything. Jesus is God in human form—the form He created us in, too. Adam was the first *human man* but he was not the first to have the form of a man. Jesus was. Because Jesus existed before Adam.

Jesus told us that only He has seen the Father. Whenever "God" in the Old Testament appeared to people as a man, it was therefore the pre-incarnate Jesus—Jesus in human form who was, and is and always will be. The Jewish people knew Him simply as "God"—not differentiating Him from the other two persons of the Trinity. The Lord God who walked and talked with Adam and Eve in the Garden of Eden was thus pre-incarnate Jesus. Before He was *born human,* Jesus had human *form.*

Male and female differences aside, there is human form. It is the form God Himself had as Jesus and the image He used when creating us. He made Eve and us in His image, formed perfectly—physically—exactly as God, the Son Himself.

We were also made perfect with qualities of God's own character, such as nurturing, a desire for relationships, creativity and love. We will explore those in future days. As Christians, we are also being *made perfect* through the working of the Holy Spirit.

> *For by one sacrifice he has made perfect forever those who are being made holy* (Hebrews 10:14).

I am as far from perfect and holy as a person can get. I continue to do the things I wish I didn't and don't do what I should. Yet I also keep hearing from Scripture that God looks at me as having been made holy and perfect in His eyes. I can almost get my brain around the idea that I have been "made acceptable." But perfect? Holy? That's hard to swallow.

> *He gave me* (Paul) *the priestly duty of proclaiming the gospel of God, so that the Gentiles might become an offering acceptable to God, sanctified* (made

> holy) *by the Holy Spirit* (Romans 15:16, explanation added).

What does *holy* mean and how can God see me that way? One definition of holy is reserved only for God: entitled to worship as if sacred—Holy God; Holy Spirit. That's Him; not us.

Holy, as it relates to us, does not mean better than anyone else as in "holier than thou." Nor does it mean without sin. To understand how God might see us as holy we have to look at other definitions:

- Belonging to a divine power
- Recognized or declared sacred by authority
- Set apart for a religious purpose

I belong to God. He—the divine power and ultimate authority—has declared me sacred. He has set me apart for His purpose. I'm holy. Like Peter said:

> *But you are a chosen people, a royal priesthood, a holy nation, a people belonging to God, that you may declare the praises of him who called you out of darkness into his wonderful light* (1 Peter 2:9).

Being good people doesn't make us holy. We can't make ourselves holy through our own power. But God can. In fact, He already has. Through Jesus' sacrifice.

> *And by that will, we have been made holy through the sacrifice of the body of Jesus Christ once for all* (Hebrews 10:10).

Being made holy through Jesus' sacrifice is beyond our understanding. Because of Jesus, in His eyes, we are now holy.

Fortunately we don't need to understand how it works. We need only accept the gift of grace and understand that—to God—we are holy. Now. In His eyes. Thanks to His doing.

Until we know Jesus, we are God's creations. When we join His family, we become children of Father God, sisters of Jesus Christ and one in Spirit. This family relationship is possible because we were made in God's image.

Squirrels and whales are God's creations, too and surely He loves them. But they are not made in His image and they are not part of His family. We were wonderfully formed in God's image, were made holy by Jesus' sacrifice, and are being perfected spiritually by the Holy Spirit.

> *Both the one who makes people holy and those who are made holy are of the same family. So Jesus is not ashamed to call them brothers and sisters* (Hebrews 2:11).

God formed Adam and Eve. We have been born. All of us have been created in Jesus' image. And then we can be born again into His spiritual life.

If Eve were here she would be able to tell us about Jesus. She knew him personally and recognized that she was made in His image. Being made in God's image is part of Eve's story. And it is part of ours.

Who are we to God? When we recognize that God created us in His perfect image and that we are being made perfect by Him, we understand how He might see His women of faith. We can answer:

I am like Eve.

For Thought and Discussion

- How do you feel about your own body, knowing that the God of the universe has a body of the same design?

- How do you feel about Jesus making you holy? What responsibility do you have to continue Jesus' work?

- How do you show thankfulness for God's gift of holiness?

PRAYER: Heavenly Father, thank you for your amazing creations. We're sorry when we take these bodies for granted or complain about them. Please remind us, Jesus, that you gave us ones that are just like yours. Thank you for loving us that much. Thank you also for continuing to work in us, Holy Spirit and for loving us through it all. Amen.

Day 3—God Breathed Life into Me

Thirty years ago I was a tornado. The things I could accomplish, amazed even me. I could clean the house, pay bills, do the laundry and finish the grocery shopping all between the time I dropped my child off at preschool and picked her up two and a half hours later. Now I have 10 hours between the time hubby leaves for work and the time he gets home and I barely finish the top three items on my to-do list. Yet by the end of the day, I have to sit down and catch my breath.

Breath. You can't live without it. And just like so many things related to God, the breath of life has three meanings: physical life, spiritual life and as it relates to Scripture.

> *Then the LORD God formed a man from the dust of the ground and breathed into his nostrils the breath of life, and the man became a living being* (Genesis 2:7).

Job tells us that God breathed life into him also.

the breath of the Almighty gives me life (Job 33:4).

God also breathed life into all the creatures He created.

> *"And to all the beasts of the earth and all the birds in the sky and all the creatures that move along the ground—everything that has the breath of life in it—I give every green plant for food." And it was so* (Genesis 2:30).

Paul tells us: *...he himself gives everyone life and breath and everything else* (Acts 17:25).

God gave the breath of life to all the beasts of the earth, the birds and every creature that moves on the ground, including us. We women are one of God's creations and we belong to Him. Our lives are made possible because He has breathed life into us. Our lives are His to do with what He wants. For His Plan. To accomplish His purpose.

> *Do you not know that your bodies are temples of the Holy Spirit, who is in you, whom you have received from God?* ***You are not your own****; you were bought at a price. Therefore honor God with your bodies* (1 Corinthians 6:19-20, emphasis added).

God didn't give us physical life for no reason. He gave us life for His reasons. It is our responsibility to use our lives in a way that honors Him; not wasting them but taking His gift and growing it so that His world is better because we have lived in it.

The breath of life can also refer to our spiritual life. Jesus came to be an example of how to live. He is the body broken for us, the blood shed for us and the living water. He is also the breath of life.

> *And when he had said this, he* (Jesus) *breathed on them and said to them, "Receive the Holy Spirit"* (John 20:22, explanation added).

In other words, God is still breathing spiritual life into us through the Holy Spirit. In fact, Jesus came so that we would not only have eternal life but that we would be able to live this life abundantly (John 10:10). The Holy Spirit empowers us to do so.

Scripture also is breath of life:

> *All Scripture is breathed out by God and profitable for teaching, for reproof, for correction, and for training in righteousness* (2 Timothy 3:15).

Reading, study and meditation of Scripture—breathed out by God Himself and made a part of our internal thinking—is also breath of life to us. In other words, if we want the spiritual breath of God to help us make more of God's physical breath of life, we need to breathe in Scripture.

If Eve were here she would acknowledge that God had breathed into her the breath of life. She didn't have Scripture, but she did have the Word of God because she talked to God in the Garden. Speaking His Word to Eve, God thus gave her not only the breath of physical life but the breath of spiritual life as well.

Who are we to God? When we accept His breath of life and breathe it for ourselves through His Spirit and pay attention to His Word, we learn that God breathes life into lifelessness. We then understand how God might see His women of faith. We can answer:

I am like Eve.

For Thought and Discussion

- What does the "breath of life" mean to you spiritually? When have you felt rejuvenated by God's breath of life?

- God created everything in the universe by speaking words. If the Bible is filled with God's words being breathed into it, how might studying Scripture continue His creation process in your life?

- God gave us life for His reasons. Our job is to be obedient. How are you doing with that? What could you do more or better? Or is there something you should be doing less or not at all?

PRAYER: Heavenly Father, thank you for giving us life and for breathing life into our hearts spiritually. Please open our minds to the teaching you have breathed into Scripture. Make our souls more fully alive in you. Amen.

Day 4—God Made Me Very Good

One day, sorting through old photographs, I discovered a black and white picture of a little girl asleep in a bed, blankets tucked under her chin, surrounded by dollies. It took a moment to recognize that the sweet little girl was me—back when I was a sweet little girl. That photograph reminded me of the innocence children are born with.

Yes, we know that children are born with Eve's original sin upon their souls. Children are self-centered and demanding. Children scream and misbehave. But still, we are born innocent of the ways of evil and have not yet had the chance to make poor choices and to fall deeply into sin.

Some days I bemoan the woman I am. I look at the mistakes I have made; the sins I have committed. I try to imagine how I could have been so immature, stupid and ignorant to have done the things I've done. And I try to imagine how God could love me though, after and in spite of all I've done.

I found myself crying as I gazed at that photograph; grieving for my loss of innocence; mourning for the child I was no more. As I bowed my head in prayer, asking God how He could love even me; even now, I clearly heard His heart to mine telling me to open my eyes and look again at the photograph in my hand. "That, dear daughter, is how I see you still."

I sin. I make mistakes. I hurt others. I hurt myself. But God didn't make me sinful. I wasn't a mistake. He didn't create me to hurt. He made me, not just good, but very good. When we come to Jesus, we become a part of God's family. And like earthly parents, our Heavenly Father, keeps a photograph of us in His spiritual wallet, sharing with pride His children; reminding us and others that He made us very good.

On day one of creation, God created light and separated it from darkness. On day two God created a vault to separate the waters and called the vault above "sky." On day three God gathered the water under the sky and created ground and vegetation on the land. For the first time in Scripture, God declared that it was good.

On day four of creation, God placed the sun, moon and stars in the sky and God saw that it was good. On day five God created creatures in the water and birds and blessed them. On day six God created creatures on the land and saw that it was good, too.

And then, still on day six, God made mankind (male and female) in His image to rule over all the creatures in the sea, sky and on the land. God blessed mankind (Genesis 1:28) and

> *God saw all that he had made, and it was **very good**. And there was evening, and there was morning—the sixth day* (Genesis 1:31, emphasis added).

Did you see it? God made all those other things. But He blessed mankind and saw that it was not just good, but *very good*. Creation wasn't *very* good until after God had made mankind and blessed us.

God only made one Eve. He also only made one woman exactly like He made you and exactly like He made me. We are each unique and have a special place in His heart and a special part to play in His plan. He made each of us very good.

If Eve were here she would agree that, as part of the brand new, fresh and untainted world God had made, He made her very good.

Who are we to God? When we recognize that God made us very good, despite our sin, we understand how God might see His women of faith. We can answer:

I am like Eve.

For Thought and Discussion

- How do you feel knowing that Scripture very definitely makes a distinction between how good mankind is from how God made fish and birds; earth and sky?

- Alternate thinking is that God's declaration refers to the cumulative effect of creation. Water, sky, land, vegetation, and creatures were good; even humans were only good. But together, God's creation was very good; implying that we are a necessary component to creation's perfection. Which interpretation do you find most comforting?

- In what ways do you struggle to see yourself as not very good or not good at all? How can you remember Genesis 1:31 to remind you of how God sees you?

PRAYER: Heavenly Father, we know that you made us and therefore we are wondrously formed. But sometimes we struggle to see that you made us very good. We often feel incapable, unlovely and unlovable. Please remind us today, Jesus, that you still see us the way you saw Eve—as your creation made perfectly as you had planned—that we are not just good; but very good in your eyes. Amen.

Day 5—I am the Jewel of God's Creation

I used to misinterpret the creation of woman as us being second-rate. Adam came first, I reasoned, so God must have believed man to be better than woman. Maybe woman was an afterthought. Then Scripture reminded me that God also made fish and birds first. Does that mean God loves fish more than He loves me? Doubtful.

The sequence of creation does not mean that the first was better than the last. God created things in order. He first created the heavens so there would be a place for the Earth. Then He separated the heavens, the water and the ground so there would be a place for the creatures He planned to put there. Then He created mankind to rule over it all.

I no longer interpret the last of creation as being the least in His eyes. But being made last does not mean better either. Rather, God created woman last and then was done. The creation of women marked the completion of creation. It's as if women were God's jewel of creation. God made everything and when He had made woman, He was done.

When we look closely at the Genesis record between chapters 1 and 2, we see something important. Something in the design sequence. Chapter 1 is an overview of creation. Chapter 2 gets more specific. In chapter 1, we see the general sequence of creation and how after God created *both* man and woman, it was very good.

Moving on to Chapter 2 and the specifics, we watch as God created man but before He created woman. He may have already *planned* to create woman. But after He had created man and before He formed woman, God declared that man alone was *not good*.

> *The LORD God said, "**It is not good** for the man to be alone. I will make a helper suitable for him"* (Genesis 2:18, emphasis added).

Women are neither an improvement over men nor an afterthought. Rather, God created both men and women exactly as He intended. But before God was done with creation—before He had formed woman—God said that circumstances were "not good." After He created woman though, it was "very good."

It's not that God saved the best for the last, although surely we're more important to Him than the fish; more beautiful than the birds; more loved than the orangutans. And we know we're superior physically to the snails because, after all, we're made in God's image and they're not. Surely in God's eyes, He made us more desirable than He made them.

But He made us all as part of His original design. He may have paused in creation before forming us women, but we were part of the plan. We're like the top jewel in the crown designed by a master jeweler; the last to be set in place. We're the cherry on the ice cream sundae, designed by the master chef. We're not an afterthought. We're not a correction. We are part of the design that completes the design.

We're the exclamation point that ends the statement: And God saw that it was very good (!)

If Eve were here she would say this was her story. She knew she was not an afterthought, nor was she of lesser or greater value than Adam in God's eyes. She did not believe herself to be better than or inferior to Adam. She simply knew that God created her. End of creation. Beginning of story.

Who are we to God? When we recognize that God created us to be a jewel of His creation design, we understand how God might see His women of faith. We can answer:

I am like Eve.

For Thought and Discussion

- How does it make you feel, knowing that as a woman, you were the very last of God's creations?

- How does it make you feel, knowing that God's design was incomplete without women? How does it make you feel loved knowing that God created everything and then placed woman into His perfect setting?

- Had you ever felt that woman was either an afterthought or an improvement? Do you now solidly recognize woman's place in God's overall design plan?

PRAYER: Heavenly Father, please remind us in a real way today how much you love and value us. Please help us understand what it means that you made us as the jewel in your creation. Amen.

Day 6—I am Different from Man

My husband is a problem solver. Like most men. When I have a problem I tell him about it because I need to vent. Like most women. I don't necessarily want Jim to solve the problem. I just need him to be an ear so I can speak the feelings stuck inside my heart, get them out and make room for the solution to emerge or the patience for the situation to resolve.

This difference between my husband and I is partly because of our personalities. But it is also a difference between men and women in general. As much as we like to determine that men and women are equal in all ways, we do not deal with things in the same way. We are, however, of equal *value* to God, as Paul tells us:

> *There is neither Jew nor Gentile, neither slave nor free, nor is there male and female, for you are all one in Christ Jesus* (Galatians 3:28).

Yesterday, we saw that God did not make Eve better or worse than Adam. Although God shows no favoritism, we are *different* from each other as genders and also as unique individuals. People also each have individual spiritual gifts.

> *We have different gifts, according to the grace given to each of us* (Romans 12:6).

No one has all of the spiritual gifts listed in Scripture. Nor do any two people with the same spiritual gifts use them in the same way. But as the church, we are expected to use them together for the greater good of all and to fulfill God's purpose.

> *For just as each of us has one body with many members, and these members do not all have the same function, so in Christ we, though many, form one body, and each member belongs to all the others* (Romans 12:4-5).

Just like the church needs each person's individual spiritual gifts, our world needs the differences between men and women for it to be a better place. Procreation notwithstanding, men and women need each other. Society needs both men and women to make it a better place. We need the insistent strength men provide; the adventurous spirit they exhibit; their courage to take chances. Our world also needs woman's inner strength, the nurturing and spiritual seeking that is part of our nature.

Men and women individually are a good thing; but we are better together. Before God formed Eve, Adam was alone and it was "not good." After woman was formed, God's creation became "very good." Yes, we have our struggles in relationships because of gender differences. But we are better as a species due to those differences. Because God made us different, humanity is richer.

We sometimes complain about those differences—grumbling how annoying men can be and how much more righteous we women are. As if. But think about this idea: what if, the very thing we dislike most about the men in our lives is part of what we love most about them?

For example: My husband has the gift of creative planning. He knows how to get us all going in new directions. Sometimes that's annoying because I'm a don't-change-things kind of gal. When Jim gets our family moving in a new direction, we're never sure how things will end up. But I love that he always looks beyond the horizon to imagine how things might be better.

From Jim's point of view, he is forever getting stumped by my now-hold-on-a-minute, feet dragging attitude. But he also loves that sometimes that attitude makes me the voice of reason for his more *creative* schemes.

Maybe something that annoys you most about men is that they always think they have the answer. But one of the great things about men is that they tend to be problem solvers in the first place. If it wasn't for men seeking to solve problems, things would be in more of an unresolved mess than ever. Left to women, all we'd do is talk about what needed doing. We may not always like the way problems are resolved, but men do have the gift of problem solving.

The very first thing God had to say about marriage is that man will leave his father and mother and be joined to woman. Although God didn't say the same thing about women, women in general also have a God-given desire to marry. Not every woman wears a white dress and strolls down the aisle. But most women grow up wanting to be married; wanting to devote their lives to one man who will love her forever. God made us that way; as a foreshadowing of what He wants for us in our relationship with Him. God wants us to be His bride—the church. Jesus, our bridegroom, will one day give us a white gown to wear and we'll live with Him forever.

God's plan may not be for every woman to marry here on earth. But one of Eve's examples for us is that God created her to be a help mate and companion.

> *So the LORD God caused the man to fall into a deep sleep; and while he was sleeping, he took one of the man's ribs and then closed up the place with flesh. Then the LORD God made a woman from the rib he had taken out of the man, and he brought her to the man.*
>
> *The man said, "This is now bone of my bones and flesh of my flesh; she shall be called 'woman,' for she was taken out of man."*
>
> *That is why a man leaves his father and mother and is united to his wife, and they become one flesh* (Genesis 2:21-24).

These verses show how vital men and women are to each other. Without Adam's rib, woman would not be here. Without sacrificing his rib, man would not have a help mate. We need each other in one-on-one relationships. We need each other in society. We need each other in the body of Christ, the church.

If Eve were here she would say this was her story. She understood that she was a help mate to Adam. He was also a help mate to her. God made Adam and Eve to need each other and help each other through life.

Who are we to God? When we recognize that we need others and that God intends us to help each other, we understand how God might see His women of faith. By sharing our gifts and the differences that make us unique, we can answer:

I am like Eve.

For Thought and Discussion

- Think about a man in your life. What one thing that you dislike about his actions or character might also be one of the very things you love about him?

- List some stereotypically female and male characteristics. How might they complement each other?

- Who in your life could you be a help mate to? Who in your life needs companionship?

PRAYER: Heavenly Father, thank you for variety in this world; even and most especially for variety among people. Please remind us to appreciate uniqueness in others, to remember that we are all part of your whole and that you have made us exactly as you desire. Amen.

My Place in God's World

Day 7—I Live Amid Incomparable Beauty

I'm not a swimmer. I don't even like to take long showers. But the very first time I ever snorkeled was a moment I will never forget. Jim and I had arrived in Hawaii. He wanted to SCUBA dive. I wanted to tag along, so I signed up on the same boat for a snorkeling trip, after being assured that—yes, I would be provided with both a life jacket and an inner tube.

We arrived at Captain Cook's Monument and Jim disappeared with his black-finned friends to explore the ocean depths. After 20 minutes' trepidation and allowing everyone else into the water first, I finally slunk my way—bulky as I was in my life jacket—into the water. I clasped hold of the boat as the grinning skipper slid the giant inner tube over my massive jacket. I ultimately let go and floated free.

Amid the shouts of "oh, look" from the paddling tourists around me, I finally affixed my goggles and snorkel and, taking an unnecessary deep breath, lowered my face into the water.

The deep breath turned out to be necessary after all because the world below me took my breath away. Immediately I pulled my feet up underneath me, grabbed my inner tube tighter and shrieked into my snorkel. I had never seen anything so foreign...and so incredibly beautiful.

The depth below me was perhaps 30 feet to the bottom—not far in oceanic terms. But the water—so clear—magnified the expanse, making it feel like miles between my dangling toes and the glorious coral. And glorious it was—rocks covered with orange and pink; blue and green. Living anemones and flora fluttered seductively in invisible currents. Rainbow fish darted beneath me singly and in groups, enticed closer by the frozen peas and carrots I offered. I can still picture the scene clearly and feel the majesty of it all deep within my soul. Fearfully and wonderfully made—God's creation was made beautiful not only for us occasional tourists, but also for the inhabitants of the watery world of the deep.

This world above sea level is beautiful, too—majestic mountains, unending planes, oceans, rivers and lakes, burbling brooks, grasslands, highlands and prairies, plateaus and pinnacles, the eerie otherworldly landscapes of the Four Corners deserts. All is beautiful not only in God's sight, but made to delight ours as well.

But all of the beauty we see around us today is but a faded image compared to the beauty God created when He set Eve down in Eden.

> *Now the LORD God had planted a garden in the east, in Eden; and there he put the man he had formed. The LORD God made all kinds of trees grow out of the ground—trees that were pleasing to the eye and good for food. In the middle of the garden were the tree of life and the tree of the knowledge of good and evil.*
>
> *A river watering the garden flowed from Eden; from there it was separated into four headwaters. The*

> *name of the first is the Pishon; it winds through the entire land of Havilah, where there is gold. (The gold of that land is good; aromatic resin and onyx are also there.) The name of the second river is the Gihon; it winds through the entire land of Cush. The name of the third river is the Tigris; it runs along the east side of Ashur. And the fourth river is the Euphrates* (Genesis 2:8-14).

The Garden of Eden held trees "pleasing to the eye." There were winding rivers and precious resources. The aromatic resin even made it smell good. It was a special place and it was beautiful.

Our world today is filled with beauty, too. In fact, God had so much beauty that He hid some. Have you ever looked through a microscope? Ever seen photos of snowflakes? Their beauty is hidden from our normal sight.

Even after God finished filling the sky with sunrises and rainbows; when He had completed the ocean with the grand and serene and adorned the land with trees and expanses, He still had beauty left. So He hid it underneath the ground. We call those bits of beauty *gold, silver, gemstones*. They are beautiful and valuable, so much so that we call them "precious."

God made Eve's first home, Eden, beautiful. He made this one beautiful. And He made heaven beautiful, too. The Book of Revelation describes the new heaven and new earth.

> *Then the angel showed me the river of the water of life, as clear as crystal, flowing from the throne of God and of the Lamb down the middle of the great street of the city. On each side of the river stood the tree of life, bearing twelve crops of fruit, yielding its fruit every month. And the leaves of the tree are for the healing of the nations* (Revelation 22:1-2).

Winding rivers, beautiful trees—including the tree of life that God had planted back in the Old Eden. The parallels to Eden and heaven are many. But in heaven we are returned to God's presence for eternity. We will be allowed to eat from the tree of life, because we will reign with Him forever.

This world, the heavens, the hidden aspects of the universe are incomparably beautiful. Yet Scripture tells us that Earth is only our temporary home. Our true and eternal home is in heaven with Him.

Jesus said he was going ahead to his Father's mansion to prepare a place for us (John 14:2). This mansion won't be like Peter's idea at the transfiguration, where Peter basically said, "Hey, here's an idea—let's put up three tents." Though earth is only a temporary home for us, God didn't just pitch a tent. He created a glorious place for us to stay. All for our enjoyment and so we can glimpse a bit of His glory in it.

If Eve were here she would say this was her story. Eve lived amid incomparable beauty.

Who are we to God? When we recognize that God made us a place of incomparable beauty to live in—both now and forever—we understand how God might see His women of faith. We can answer:

I am like Eve.

For Thought and Discussion

- Where's the most beautiful place on earth you've ever visited? The ocean? The mountains? The desert? What was it that struck you so profoundly?

- Think about tiny beauties that—taken together—can overwhelm you—such as ice crystals covering trees, or the delicate petals of a rose. What one tiny thing in nature helps you see God's glory?

- What is your image of heaven?

PRAYER: Dear Jesus, thank you so much for creating beauty in this world. Please open our eyes to see more beauty around us. Please also remind us that when we see something beautiful in this world, it is a reflection of you. Amen.

Day 8—I Have Stewardship over the Earth

Today I planned to write this chapter about taking care of God's world. As my computer was waking itself up, I headed downstairs to get coffee. Before leaving the room, I flipped the light switch to *on* so the room would be ready when I returned. I walked two steps out of the room, remembered what chapter I would be working on and flipped the switch off. Turning on a light just as I'm *leaving* the room is definitely not an example of wise stewardship of God's energy.

> *Then God said, "Let us make mankind in our image, in our likeness, so that they may rule over the fish in the sea and the birds in the sky, over the livestock and all the wild animals, and over all the creatures that move along the ground"* (Genesis 1:26).

Everything in the universe belongs to God. But He gave stewardship over the earth to Adam and Eve. That stewardship flows also to us. We are stewards of the earth; not just to enjoy, but to manage for Him; to keep safe; to make better. How am I doing, managing His world for Him? This morning I had to admit that I wasn't doing very well.

In Matthew, Jesus' parable of the three servants taking care of the master's money illustrates how God expects us to be good stewards of God's world, including the people He has placed in our lives and the tangible blessings God has given us personally. It also means we have a responsibility to take care of these bodies we call "ours." They, too belong to God, as do our very souls. God has only allowed us to take care of these things on His behalf. And it all started back in the Garden.

> *The earth is the LORD's, and everything in it, the world, and all who live in it* (Psalm 24:1).

The universe belongs to God. But God gave Adam and Eve responsibility for taking care of the earth and everything in it (and presumably everything beyond the earth we can access). That responsibility flows from Adam and Eve to us.

When we leave lights on in rooms we aren't using, yes, we pay the electric bill but the electricity and the resources used to create it belong to God. When we let the water run down the drain while we get a towel, yes we pay the water bill but the water is God's resource and His resources are used to recycle that water and make it available for the next person. If we are wasting it, are we being good stewards of God's stuff?

Stewardship extends to us as well. If we are not taking care of our bodies; if we are wasting our time and our talents; our love and our joy, are we being good stewards of God's stuff?

We have exceptional medicine and the means to obtain it. We have unlimited food, clean water, and the education to know what we should do to maintain these bodies. Yet health in the Western world gets worse each year. How do you think God is looking at the job we're doing of taking care of His stuff—our bodies?

We have an abundance of free time. How many of us waste our time on television programs or social media? How do you think God is looking at the job we're doing of taking care of His stuff—our time and talents?

What about the people God has placed in our lives? Are we good stewards of them as well?

> *See to it that no one falls short of the grace of God and that no bitter root grows up to cause trouble and defile many* (Hebrews 12:15).

The New Living Translation says to "look after each other" so that no one fails to receive the grace of God. The New Testament calls us to look after widows and orphans. We are to love one another. We are to practice hospitality.

God has blessed us with family members. He desires us to be responsible for them. He has placed friends and acquaintances in our lives. He has placed us in neighborhoods and businesses where we meet people. He has given us stewardship over these people to a certain extent. If nothing else, He has made us responsible for doing what we can to share His love for them.

The very last words recorded from Jesus are referred to as "The Great Commission."

> *"Therefore go and make disciples of all nations, baptizing them in the name of the Father and of the Son and of the Holy Spirit, and teaching them to obey everything I have commanded you"* (Matthew 28:19).

Jesus did not give everyone responsibility for teaching people to become Christ-like. But He has given all believers the responsibility for introducing people to Him and telling them the good news—that God has provided a way for all of us to once again return to living in His presence.

Jesus clearly commissioned all believers to introduce people to Him—to share His message with the world. How do you think God is looking at the job we're doing taking care of His stuff—our faith?

If Eve were here she would say this was her story. God gave her stewardship of the world and everything in it. She had to learn personally that stewardship included staying away from what was forbidden.

Who are we to God? When we recognize that God expects us to take care of His resources and the people and things He has blessed us with, as well as to avoid what God tells us to avoid for our own good, we understand how God might see His women of faith. We can answer:

I am like Eve.

For Thought and Discussion

- Who in your life do you have stewardship over? Who has stewardship over you? How are you doing with that responsibility? How are they doing?

- How has God spoken to you about the Great Commission? How have you responded to that commission? If you haven't, how might you begin?

- What aspects of stewardship over God's resources are you most passionate about? How might you work at pursuing that passionate stewardship in a practical way?

PRAYER: Heavenly Father, thank you for allowing us to take care of your world and the people you have placed in it. Thank you especially for making us stewards of our faith. Help us be good stewards in all things; but especially help us be bold and share your good news with others. Amen.

Day 9—I Can't Hide from God

Our daughter was the best player in every game of hide and seek. Not because she found hiding places no one else could find but because she could *fit* into hiding places no one else could. So no one bothered to look for her there—such as the cabinet underneath the bathroom sink and inside the clothes hamper. On the other hand, every time our son hid, we knew exactly where he was. All we had to do was follow the sound of his giggling. The hard part was pretending not to know he was there.

> *Then the man and his wife heard the sound of the LORD God as he was walking in the garden in the cool of the day, and they hid from the LORD God among the trees of the garden. But the LORD God called to the man, "Where are you?"*
>
> *He answered, "I heard you in the garden, and I was afraid because I was naked; so I hid"* (Genesis 3:8-10).

I love those verses. Adam and Eve hid among the trees of the Garden. As if God couldn't find them there. Adam and Eve had just covered themselves with leaves. Did they imagine they had perfect camouflage? Dressed for guerilla warfare in the battle between good and evil?

I can practically hear Adam whisper to Eve. "Duck! God will never find us here."

As if.

All knowing. All seeing God. But look at what a gentleman God was. God called to the man, "Where are you?" Ollie, Ollie oxen free! Come out, come out wherever you are.

Come to me all who are weary and I will give you rest.

Sometimes hiding from God has to do with hiding from guilt, like Adam and Eve did. Sometimes hiding from God has to do with trying to avoid His leading.

Have you ever felt God leading you to do something? Take on a ministry? Reach a person for Him? Be obedient in an area of your life? Have you tried to avoid His leading? Maybe you tried to argue with God, saying you weren't the right person; didn't have the time or resources; someone else would be better suited. Or maybe you heard His leading and didn't respond at all except with great, engulfing silence.

Yes, God could get someone else to complete His plan. He could do it Himself without any help at all. But if the God of the universe wants you or me to participate in His eternal project? Wow. Even if I'm afraid. Even if I don't think I'm up to it. Even if I don't think I want to do it. If God thinks I can? That's pretty darned cool. I want to shout: I may not be ready, God, but ready or not, here I come!

Most of the people whose lives are recorded in Scripture were major screw-ups. But God used them. We're imperfect, too. And usually we're not perfectly prepared. But when we provide the willing heart to be God's hands and feet in the world, we can trust that God will provide the tools, talent, time, resources, knowledge and people we need to finish the job.

God knows where we are, what we are doing and what we need. But He politely calls out to us and asks us to come to Him, naked though we are.

When we accept Jesus into our lives, we get the gift of the Holy Spirit's presence. God is with us always. That's one more way He knows where we are and what we are doing. We can't hide from Him. And He loves us even when we try.

If Eve were here she would say this was her story. She couldn't hide from God.

Who are we to God? When we realize we can't hide from God and decide that it is better not to try, we understand how God might see His women of faith. We can answer:

I am like Eve.

For Thought and Discussion

- How does it make you feel knowing the Holy Spirit is with you at all times? How does that knowledge affect your thinking about hiding from God?

- Have you ever tried to hide from God? How did that work? What happened when you stopped trying to hide? Or do you still need to come out of hiding?

- How might you help someone else get past trying to hide from God?

PRAYER: Heavenly Father, thank you for loving us so much that you love us even when we try to hide from you. Thank you, Jesus, for calling out to us to come into your presence. And thank you, Holy Spirit, for being with us always. Amen.

Day 10—God is Looking for Me

Every house in my neighborhood has a doorbell. So why does someone come to my door and knock quietly? So as not to disturb me? If you don't want to disturb me, then go away and leave me alone. But if you want to talk with me, ring the doorbell and wait. I'll be there in a sec.

Yep, that's me being petty. In reality, maybe my visitor wonders if I have a sleeping baby in my home. Maybe they're trying not to alarm the dogs. Maybe they just are trying to be soft and gentle of spirit.

Like Jesus.

Yesterday, we saw that Eve tried to hide from God. The point today is that just as God was looking for Eve, Jesus is looking for us today.

> *Here I am! I stand at the door and knock. If anyone hears my voice and opens the door, I will come in and eat with that person, and they with me* (Revelation 3:20).

God seeks us out and then stands at the door and knocks. He doesn't bang. He doesn't use a crow bar. He doesn't even ring the doorbell. He stands at the door and knocks. He wants us to seek Him. But whatever seeking of Him we do or do not do, He has never stopped seeking us.

Sometimes God uses major events in our lives to get our attention. A birth or an illness; a crisis or an unexpected blessing is more obvious than a gentle tap-tap-tapping on our hearts. Some of us need Jesus to ring the doorbell or blow a horn or flip the switch on the siren before we even notice He's at our door; much less that we recognize He wants into our hearts.

Once we have opened the door to Jesus and let Him in though, He still isn't done seeking us. He desires not only that none be lost but also that we grow in the depth of our relationship with Him. Jesus seeks not just to give us salvation but to enrich our lives through Him and to help us grow more into His likeness so that others may see Him in our lives as we stand alongside Him at their doors. As Jesus said:

> *"In the same way, let your light shine before others, that they may see your good deeds and glorify your Father in heaven"* (Matthew 5:16).

Yesterday we discussed how even if we are trying to hide, God is actively looking for us. Just like he looked for Eve in the Garden, He desires that none should be lost.

> *The Lord is not slow in keeping his promise, as some understand slowness. Instead he is patient with you, not wanting anyone to perish, but everyone to come to repentance* (2 Peter 3:9).

We may try to hide from God. We can't. He knows where we are and He is there with us, standing at the door of our hearts, knocking softly. I personally need to remember the character of Jesus when someone knocks at my door rather than rings the doorbell. Maybe it's Jesus' way of reminding me that He came to save everyone; not just me but the person at my front door, too.

But even once we have come to Jesus, He still desires our seeking. God wants to be known—as much as our humanity allows us to know God. He seeks us and desires us to seek Him.

> *Come near to God and he will come near to you* (James 4:8).

God coming near to us? Yes, that is a blessing, to be sure. The tweaky little thing about this is: God is looking for us, but He desires *us* to find *Him*. Fortunately He makes it easy. He's right there, standing at the door of our hearts, knocking softly and calling to us. And while Jesus is standing at the door knocking, He expects us to knock back.

> *"Ask and it will be given to you; seek and you will find;* ***knock and the door will be opened to you****. For everyone who asks receives; the one who seeks finds; and to the one who knocks, the door will be opened"* (Matthew 7:7-8, emphasis added).

Jesus stands at the door and knocks. He wants us to stand at the door and knock, too. He seeks us. He wants us to seek Him, too. In other words, He wants us to be with Him—on the same side of the door—with nothing between us. Found. And loved.

The very first book of the New Testament (Matthew 7:7-8) and the very last book of the New Testament (Revelation 3:20) both contain statements from Jesus. In both Scriptures Jesus tells us there is a door between us. He stands on one side; we stand on the other. He's knocking on one side and wants us to knock on the other side. The important thing is that the door open so we can be on the same side with Him.

If Eve were here she would say this was her story. In the Garden, she not only knew she couldn't hide from God. She also knew He was looking for her and ultimately let Him find her.

Who are we to God? When we recognize that God continually seeks our hearts and desires us to seek Him, we understand how God might see His women of faith. We can answer:

I am like Eve.

For Thought and Discussion

- How did God first approach you—knocking gently or pounding? Looking back, can you see He may have knocked gently at first?

- Do you still feel God pursuing your heart? In what way?

- How do you seek God?

PRAYER: Heavenly Father, thank you for desiring a relationship with us. Thank you for not giving up on what you want for us. Please help us be more attuned to you, Holy Spirit so we can more easily draw near to you. Amen.

Day 11—I Live in God's Presence

I do my very best praying while I walk. I hitch puppy dog to her leash, slide into my walking shoes and head up the street. I start out with the general, all-purpose praying topics—gratitude, praise, maybe sing a portion of a hymn that comes to mind, then pray for family and friends, projects and concerns.

It's after all of *my* prayers though, that the real praying begins—when I relinquish my praying over to the Holy Spirit; after I have said "Amen" and then added, "So, Holy Spirit, what would *you* like me to pray about?" And off we go.

What I love about this praying is that it's an adventure. I'm usually surprised at for whom or for what I end up praying. But then, God's desires are bigger than mine; God's heart breaks over things I'm not even aware of. This miracle—walking with God, living with God in me, being led by Him—is one of those blessings we never get used to and are always in awe of.

After my walk, I'll head home, and I'm sorry to say, I become oblivious to the presence of the Holy Spirit, *until* I again stop, take time to recognize His presence and re-align my thoughts so that I am open to His leading.

Then the man and his wife heard the sound of the LORD God as he was walking in the garden in the cool of the day (Genesis 3:8).

How awesome it must have been for Eve, with God walking around in the Garden. But we need not be envious of Eve. Although Eve may have been able to walk physically with God in the Garden, we can walk with God every moment of every day because Jesus made a way for us to return to the spiritual garden with Him. When the Holy Spirit lives within us, we can walk daily with God. We need to attune our thoughts and hearts to His presence in our lives. But even when we don't, He is still right there, right here, with us.

Meditation on Scripture, prayer, and teaching helps us know the character of God better. And the better we know Him, the more easily we can tune our spiritual radios to His frequency. Is this tuning a part of God's refining; of His making us perfect until the day of Christ when we walk in His very presence in heaven? How awesome would it be to always, in every instance be aware of God's presence?

Jesus became human and was called Emanuel, which means *God with us.* We sing Christmas carols about Baby Jesus being God with us. By leaving us the Holy Spirit though, Jesus gave us a way to still know Him as Emanuel. God is still with us, living in us, guiding and directing our lives to the extent and as we are able to understand.

If Eve were here, she would say that living in God's presence was her story.

Who are we to God? When we recognize that we too can live in His presence and when we seek to do so, we understand how God might see His women of faith. We can answer:

I am like Eve.

For Thought and Discussion

- Name some ways in which you are aware each day of God's presence in your life.

- Think about a time you were certain of God's presence. How did that make you feel? How can you share that experience with others?

- How might it change your life if you could see Jesus standing next to you all of the time? How can you use that image to attune your heart to God's presence daily?

PRAYER: Heavenly Father, thank you for being with us each moment of each day. Please help us attune our hearts and minds to your leading, Holy Spirit, and be more aware of your presence today. Amen.

Sin and Judgment

Day 12—I Sin

It's easy to be self-righteous; harder to get the self out of the way and just be righteous. It's comforting to jot down sins and organize them in order of horribleness to see where we fit in. As if that's what God does.

Scripture doesn't tell us that one sin is just as bad as another sin to God. Scripture does tell us that the result of every *unforgiven sin* is the same: damnation. Conversely, the result of forgiveness through Christ is the same: grace and mercy. Every time. All sin is equal in one sense: it is all disobedience to God.

> *If anyone, then, knows the good they ought to do and doesn't do it, it is sin for them* (James 4:17).

That was Eve's trouble. She knew the good she was supposed to do (obey God and not eat the forbidden fruit). But she disobeyed. That disobedience was sin.

God originally made mankind without sin. God also created the heavenly beings. Lucifer was an angel of high authority on the heavenly angel team. But then Lucifer rebelled.

So God—as is God's way—changed Lucifer's name to Satan and cast him down from heaven, "to the ground" (Isaiah 14: 12).

Out of heaven, Satan entered the Garden as a snake, bringing evil into God's perfect world. When Adam and Eve succumbed to Satan's temptation, they sinned. That sin of disobedience to God became part of mankind's nature. We all bear the consequence of that very first, original sin.

God knew evil would enter the perfect, sinless world He created when He cast Satan out of heaven. We don't understand why God thought that was the thing to do, but He did and the rest of the history of mankind is about how God is making something good come from mankind's first, original sin.

The "making something good" took a while—from our human perspective. One of the beautiful things about the Book of Leviticus is it shows that there is no sin that God didn't provide a way to cover. Sin unintentionally? Sacrifice a young bull (Leviticus 4:1-3). You didn't testify? Sacrifice a female lamb (Leviticus 5:1-6). On and on go the sin-rectifying-sacrificial rules. The Book of Leviticus proves that God had our backs to enable us to cover our sins, even before Jesus was born on earth.

But those animal sacrifices didn't allow for forgiveness of sin. They only covered the sins over, like whitewash. They did nothing to take away the stain from a person's soul. Not even a person's own blood could do that because a sacrifice required innocent blood. By definition, a sinner's blood is not innocent. Since animals were innocent though, they could die in place of the sinner.

But animal sacrifices were only a temporary fix. Sacrificing one goat—even one goat per person—was insufficient to cover all the sins humans committed. Sacrifices had to be done for each new sin and each new sinner.

Jesus though was sinless. Therefore His innocent human blood could cover sin. But then God went a step further—to address not just a *covering of sin* but complete *forgiveness*. Here's the tough theology:

Only God can forgive sin.

Only God is sinless.

Only God is worthy of Himself.

Only a sacrifice *of* God can provide the sacrifice worthy of God's own forgiveness of sins against Himself.

Fortunately God is also infinite. He never runs out of Himself. Therefore, only sinless, infinite Jesus, as God, sacrificing His infinite self, one time on the cross, provided an adequate (infinitely worthy) sacrifice to not only cover sin, but to forgive all sins for all people for all time.

> *For this is my blood of the new testament, which is shed for many for the remission* (forgiveness) *of sins* (Matthew 26:28, definition added).

Blood is the payment God requires. Scripture does not tell us why; only that life blood is the proper payment for life.

> *Without the shedding of blood, there is no forgiveness* (Hebrews 9:22).

> *"For the life of the flesh is in the blood: and I have given it to you upon the altar to make an atonement for your souls: for it is the blood that maketh an atonement for the soul"* (Leviticus 17:11).

> *For the wages of sin is death, but the gift of God is eternal life in Christ Jesus our Lord* (Romans 6:23).

Sin is death. Forgiveness of sin brings life eternal. Life is in the blood. We may not know why God required blood sacrifice, but we don't need to know. God required a blood sacrifice for sin from the very beginning of history when He sacrificed two of His animals to make clothing for Adam and Eve, thus *covering their shame and covering their sin*. And then Jesus came and finished the matter for us forever.

> *The blood of goats and bulls and the ashes of a heifer sprinkled on those who are ceremonially unclean sanctify them so that they are outwardly clean. How much more, then, will the blood of Christ, who through the eternal Spirit offered himself unblemished to God, cleanse our consciences from acts that lead to death, so that we may serve the living God!* (Hebrews 9:13-14)

The Jewish people had been taught that one day a Messiah would become their Savior. Until then, they knew only that blood covered sin. An animal, often a perfect lamb, was sacrificed in order to cover sin, recognizing that complete forgiveness was impossible. That is the importance behind what John the Baptist (a Jew) tells us when he saw Jesus.

> *"Look, the lamb of God* (God's own sacrifice) *who takes away* (not just covers) *the sin of the world"* (everyone)*!* (John 1:29, explanation added)

Jesus provided God (Himself) with His own sacrifice of Himself. We have no need for animal sacrifices that merely "cover" sins. Now our sins can be completely forgiven and the stain on our souls washed away. But first we must ask for forgiveness, repent and accept Jesus' sacrifice. We must take ownership of the very fact that we sin.

If Eve were here, she would say this was her story. Eve understood she had sinned by disobeying God. She did not have Jesus' salvation through His own sacrifice to rely on but she knew God provided her with a blood sacrifice of His own creatures to cover her shame.

Who are we to God? When we recognize we sin but that God has provided a way not just to cover our sins but to completely wash them away by the blood of Jesus, we understand how God might see His women of faith. We can answer:

I am like Eve.

For thought and discussion

- As your faith deepens, in what new areas of your life has God led you to seek forgiveness? Have your eyes been opened to things you now see as sinful that you didn't view as sinful when your faith was newer?

- In what ways have you felt completely forgiven? Do you still struggle with forgiveness in certain areas of life?

- How has an understanding of your sinful nature affected your relationships with other people? What is your forgiveness quotient with others?

PRAYER: Heavenly Father, we know you made mankind perfect and sin free but that you also allowed evil to enter this world. We're sorry when we sin. Thank you for forgiving us and loving us through it all. Please don't give up on us but keep working in our hearts to become more like you, Jesus. Amen.

Day 13—I Know God's Judgment is Good

My son was born after a cesarean section. I had no labor, but after he was born, I had another nine months of recovery from the surgery. When my daughter was born, there was no surgery. Yes, I had labor, but after it was done, I held her in my arms and declared: "Now *that* is the way to have a baby." Recovery was a few days. In both cases, although I remember the pain clearly, and in both cases the pain was pretty bad, what I remember most is that it was all worth it.

Any woman who has ever had a child can give you a play-by-play of childbirth. But nearly every story about the horrors of childbirth ends with a story of gladness when a child is the result.

Sometimes we hear people say that God cursed Adam and Eve because of their sin. But a careful reading of Scripture reveals an important truth: God did not curse mankind. God cursed the serpent and God cursed the ground. God judged and punished Adam and Eve.

> *So the* Lord *God said to the serpent, "Because you have done this, "**Cursed are you above all livestock*** (Genesis 3:14, emphasis added).

> *"**Cursed is the ground** because of you; through painful toil you will eat food from it all the days of your life* (Genesis 3:17, emphasis added).

God's punishment to Adam was painful toil of the ground. But God attached a blessing to Adam's judgment. He would have food to eat from his toil. To Eve, God said:

> *"I will make your pains in childbearing very severe; with painful labor you will give birth to children. Your desire will be for your husband, and he will rule over you"* (Genesis 3:16).

God's punishment to women was pain in childbirth. But the joy that comes from bearing that pain is an example of how God works in our lives and in our circumstances. Womankind's punishment comes with a blessing attached to it.

> *A woman giving birth to a child has pain because her time has come; but when her baby is born she forgets the anguish because of her joy that a child is born into the world* (John 16:21).

There are various interpretations about God's statement that woman's desire will be for her husband and he will rule over her. Some theologians say God intended for woman to be subject to man. Others say it is linked to the pain of childbirth—that woman will desire man sexually and the result of fulfilling that desire will be pregnancy and the pain of childbirth. Others say that this was not part of God's judgment but rather a caution against idolatry; that woman's desire for a husband and children is so strong that it may overtake her desire to know and love God Himself.

Regardless of how we interpret the "desire for our husband" portion of God's judgment, the beauty and wonder is how His judgment reflects His character. The very first book of the Bible shows us a great, big, giant insight into God. God gave Eve a punishment and a hardship for all women to bear. But that hardship came with a blessing in the form of children. For individual women, having a child may not be a joy. But a child is *meant* to be. The bearing of children is physically and emotionally hard. But the blessing is intended to last a lifetime.

Not every woman will know the pain of childbirth or the joy of having a child. Every woman will, however, know hardship at some time in her life. What God taught Eve was that He works through all things for His good purpose and works for the good in all things.

As part of God's judgment, women must bear the hardship of having children and raising them. We must work at nurturing our relationship with our husbands. We must seek to overcome idolatry when our husband and children take precedence in our lives over our love for God. Fortunately, with those hardships can come joy, even if the joy is merely the joy of knowing that God intends good for us. We may not understand His plan but we can know that it is good because He is good. And He loves us just as He loved his first daughter, Eve.

If Eve were here, she would say this was her story. She would acknowledge that she learned something important about God's character: even God's punishment came with a blessing.

Who are we to God? When we recognize we have hardships in our lives but that God can work them for our good, we understand how God might see His women of Faith. We can answer:

I am like Eve.

For Thought and Discussion

- If you have children, how vividly do you remember childbirth? Was it worth it?

- If you do not have children, have they been a desire? Not having children can also be a soul-level pain dealing with childbirth. How have you or someone you know dealt with that pain?

- Think of a hardship in your life. Did it come with a blessing? Or joy afterwards? Might it have come with a blessing you were not able to understand? Can you ask God to reveal such a blessing to you now?

PRAYER: Heavenly Father, thank you for physically making us women. We are grateful for the gift of children to this world as a reminder that you are the giver of life and that sometimes joy comes even through pain. Amen.

Day 14—I am Loved Despite My Sins

As a child, I looked at the Eve story and couldn't figure out what the big deal was. So she ate an apple. I eat apples all the time. They're full of fiber and vitamins. An apple a day—and all that. I couldn't understand how eating one piece of God's fruit could make Him so upset that the rest of mankind was doomed forever.

Yes, I *know* the forbidden fruit wasn't actually an apple.

It took me a while to get over being angry at Eve for ruining the whole "living in Eden" gig. But ultimately I recognized that God had a handle on things and had a plan to make all things work for the good for those who love Him. And since I do love Him, I do firmly believe that it was all good.

Besides, how can I condemn Eve for nibbling on a piece of tantalizing fruit after being told to do so by one of God's creations? After all, I have God's rules written down in a book, sitting next to me that I read every day and profess to believe—yet I still disobey and still sin. *For what I want to do I do not do, but what I hate I do* (Romans 7:15).

Sigh.

When Eve disobeyed God and ate from the tree of knowledge of good and evil, He proved His justice by giving her a consequence to her action. She was forced from the Garden. But before she left, God proved His love to her in a concrete, practical way she could understand at her human level. When Eve learned about good and evil, her nakedness caused her shame. The animal God sacrificed not only covered Eve's sin, it created clothing to cover her nakedness.

> *The LORD God made garments of skin for Adam and his wife and clothed them* (Genesis 3:21).

God proved His love for us definitively through Jesus' sacrifice. This act of love will become concrete for us when we step into heaven. And we only get to step into heaven at all because of grace.

The Hebrews tried to cover their sins by sacrificing animals. But nothing they did; nothing we can ever do on our own can take away our sins. And nothing we can do on our own can earn our way to heaven. We are only forgiven and only allowed heavenly citizenship because Jesus provided the only sacrifice acceptable to the Father—a sacrifice of Himself.

Yesterday, we looked at how hardship often comes with a blessing. Jesus explained this in his Sermon on the Mount (Matthew 5:1-12). Blessed are we—when we understand our sinful nature, our weakness, our grief and our shortcomings. We can do nothing on our own to earn salvation. We sin. God saves. We are blessed. Each and every one of the blessings from the Sermon on the Mount relates back to God's grace.

Blessed are the poor in spirit. Our spirits are poor. Only because of God's grace are we made rich spiritually.

Blessed are they who mourn. We mourn because we have no hope outside of Christ. We mourn for those who are lost forever. But God's grace comforts us.

Blessed are the meek. We cannot demand salvation. We can only accept God's gift of grace. When we do—as adopted children of God—we inherit His kingdom and also inherit the New Earth on the day of Christ.

Blessed are those who hunger and thirst for righteousness. When we desire God above all, He will fill us.

Blessed are the merciful. When we forgive and have mercy for others, God will bless us with His mercy.

Blessed are the pure in heart. When we recognize we can only be pure in heart when we allow God to purify us; when we pursue a relationship with Jesus, we will be able to glimpse God.

Blessed are those who are persecuted because of righteousness. When we stand up for what God stands for, God recognizes us as one of His own. We are blessed to be received into His kingdom. Forever.

The Beatitudes are recognitions of how much we need God. They are recognitions of how far we are from perfect; how far sin has taken us from God's presence and how every gram of righteousness we might claim comes through Jesus. But the Beatitudes also encourage us with the knowledge that when we lean into God, we are blessed, because we are loved. Each hardship comes with a blessing.

There was another blessing that came with God's original punishment that proves His eternal love for us. When God sent Adam and Eve out of the Garden, He set cherubim to guard the tree of life so Adam and Eve could not eat from it and live forever. Although that sounds bad, it was eternally good.

God's justice sent Adam and Eve away from the Garden. Without the tree of life to nourish them, Adam and Eve could no longer be immortal (live on earth forever without dying.) Adam and Eve could only return to God, by dying and entering Heaven, safe from Satan forever. The blessing part of God's punishment was that mortal death provided a way for Eve to return to Him. In essence, God upgraded mankind's status from immortal beings to eternal beings.

If Eve were here, she would say this was her story. Eve understood she had sinned. She also knew though that God had never stopped loving her. He provided for her as she left the Garden and He provided for her to be with Him eternally.

Who are we to God? When we recognize that God loves us eternally even though we sin, we can understand how God might see His women of faith. We can answer:

I am like Eve.

For Thought and Discussion

- What are some of the everyday, practical blessings you see coming from God?

- How do you feel understanding that we can do nothing on our own to ensure salvation?

- What new insights do you have about the Beatitudes? How can you apply them?

PRAYER: Heavenly Father, thank you so much for loving us, sinful as we are. Thank you for continuing to provide for our needs. Thank you that your love and forgiveness are completely dependent only on your character and not on anything we could do on our own. Amen.

Day 15—God's Rules are for My Good

Back in the days before Jesus, those poor Hebrews had so many rules and regulations—do this; don't do that; don't do it after sundown on Friday and really don't do it on these special days of the year. And that was *after* God had already given them the big Ten Commandments.

But in the Garden, God didn't give Eve a pile of rules. He gave her just one—do not eat from the tree of knowledge of good and evil. That rule was definitely for her good. God told her if she ate the fruit, she would surely die.

Evidently God didn't intend the fruit to be poison, because when Eve ate the fruit she didn't suddenly shrivel up. Rather because she disobeyed that rule, the consequence was that God no longer allowed her to eat from that *other* tree in the Garden—the tree of life. If Adam and Eve could not eat from the tree of life, the result is that they would die a mortal death. God spoke the truth: *they would surely die*, because the consequence of disobedience was inaccessibility to the tree of life-giving fruit.

God's rule was for Eve's good.

God has a lot of rules about food. Many theologians speculate as to some of the odd rules in the books of Moses (Genesis, Exodus, Leviticus, Numbers and Deuteronomy). Some rules seem arbitrary, while others apparently are generally good guidelines for living a good life or to provide a healthy environment for a society on the move as the Jews were. Some historians speculate that certain dietary restrictions had to do with protecting people from health hazards. This thinking is supported by Scripture:

> *He (the LORD) said, "If you listen carefully to the LORD your God and do what is right in his eyes, if you pay attention to his commands and keep all his decrees,* ***I will not bring on you any of the diseases*** *I brought on the Egyptians, for I am the LORD, who heals you"* (Exodus 15:26, explanation and emphasis added).

By the time the early Christians received Peter's revelation 2000 years later that all food was acceptable in God's eyes, historians speculate that healthier crop and animal raising no longer required as strict dietary guidelines to maintain the health of society. But, when looking at dietary guidelines from God's perspective, He has not changed His rules but has moved us forward step by step. In the Garden, God told Adam and Eve they could eat what grew on the trees (except that one tree) and all seed-bearing plants.

> *Then God said, "I give you every seed-bearing plant on the face of the whole earth and every tree that has fruit with seed in it. They will be yours for food" (Genesis 1:29).*

After the flood, God extended mankind's dietary bounty to "everything that lives and moves about" (Genesis 9:3). When the

Hebrew's lifestyle and circumstances changed after they left Egypt, their diets were clarified by God through Moses. Then Jesus came and everything became acceptable (Acts 10:9-13).

The important thing to remember is that God's rules are for our good. They are important for a reason. Even if that reason is not clear to us from our modern, human perspective. The main, number one rule though has always been the same and is reflected in the fact that four out of the Ten Commandments refer to our relationship with God. King Solomon figured it out and Eve ultimately did, too:

> *Fear and love God and obey His commandments; for this is the sole purpose of man* (Ecclesiastes 12:13).

We are to fear and love God and obey His commandments. Eve hid from God when she disobeyed God's rule. When God found Adam and Eve they stood before God. Eve blamed the serpent and Adam blamed "the woman" God gave her (essentially blaming God Himself). But they then accepted God's judgment and left the Garden.

If Eve were here today, she would say this was her story. She learned that God's rules were for her good.

Who are we to God? When we recognize that God's loving rules are for our good even if we don't understand them, we know how God might see His women of faith. We can answer:

I am like Eve.

For Thought and Discussion

- Do you have dietary restrictions that are for your good? How do you feel about them? Do you follow them?

- Are there any rules in the Bible that you don't understand why they are there? Do you think the Jews understood the reasoning behind every rule?

- Were you raised with house rules you didn't understand as a child? Did you ultimately recognize that they were for your good?

PRAYER: Heavenly Father, forgive our rebelliousness. Our independent spirit sometimes makes us resist your rules, even when we understand they are for our good. Please forgive us and remind us that what you desire for us is only good. Amen.

I Learn from My Mistakes

Day 16—I Recognize Good and Evil

Our family loves action movies—explosions, car chases and flying bullets. We even enjoy a good disaster and the occasional zombie movie. But I cannot watch movies where the antagonist is Satan.

A gunfight can be won. A disaster can be overcome. Those stories are about mankind's ability to persevere. But there is nothing we mortals can do to fight evil. All we can do is stay as far away from it as we can and seek protection from God.

Eve sinned. That was bad. Eve ate the forbidden fruit. That was bad. Eve no longer could live in the Garden, could no longer eat from the tree of life, and could no longer live forever. Those were all bad consequences. But by allowing Eve to die, God provided a way for Eve to return to Him in heaven, safe from evil.

Eating the forbidden fruit gave Eve understanding of the difference between good and evil. Afterwards, she could see evil around her and recognized how evil affected her personally. That's a blessing that came from her sin. By recognizing evil, she could seek God's protection from it.

Because of Eve, we also have the ability to know when what we are doing is wrong. Having that knowledge isn't pleasant. It's scary to see evil around us. It's painful when we recognize sin within ourselves. But seeking God's protection and repenting can bring us closer to God. That's a good thing.

Eve sinned. A blessing part of God's judgment was that her sin gave humanity the ability to recognize good and evil, right at the beginning when evil first entered the world. We know how to recognize evil because we can compare everything to God's standard. Not to judge others, but to learn so we can grow more into Jesus' likeness.

God didn't make us infallible. He made us teachable. He wants us to learn, even—and maybe especially—when things go terribly wrong in our lives. When we see evil tendencies within ourselves, we can turn away from evil and turn toward God. We can recognize our sins and learn from our mistakes. We can turn to the source of all good.

No matter how righteous we try to be, we all sin. God wants us to see our sins and recognize them for what they are. But until we are in a proper relationship with God, sometimes we are not able to see them as God does. Fortunately, Jesus provided a way to be forgiven. Not only do we need to seek His forgiveness though. God also wants us to turn away from our sins and toward Him. That too, is part of the forgiveness equation.

There is sin in this world—us people failing to obey God. Separately from sin, there is also evil—brought into this world by Satan. When Eve ate from the tree of knowledge of good and evil, she was able to recognize good and evil.

Because Eve's original sin has fallen on us, we also can recognize good and evil in the world. We can compare everything, every circumstance, every person, every action to God. We sin, but God did not make us evil. The blessing that came from God's judgment of Eve's original sin is that we can be on the lookout for evil, recognize it and turn toward God for protection and guidance.

After Eve was banished from Eden, God's other instruction to Adam and Eve had been:

> *"Be fruitful and increase in number; fill the earth and subdue it. Rule over the fish in the sea and the birds in the sky and over every living creature that moves on the ground"* (Genesis 2:28).

Evidently Eve and Adam did a good enough job being fruitful and ruling over the creatures, because mankind and planet Earth survived. Evidently Eve had learned from her mistake and moved forward to follow God's instructions.

Who are we to God? When we learn from our mistakes, turn away from evil and toward God, we understand how God might see His women of faith. We can answer:

I am like Eve.

For Thought and Discussion

- Recall when your faith was new. What sins did God reveal to you about your character? What about now?

- Is there a sin you presently struggle with? How can you focus on turning away from that sin and turning toward God? How do you reconcile continuing to accept God's grace with His desire that you turn away from sin?

- How do you recognize evil in the world? How do you protect yourself from it?

PRAYER: Heavenly Father, thank you for loving us even when we sin. Please shine a light into our hearts and illuminate any dark places you see there. Please help us turn away from sin and turn toward you. Please protect us from evil always. Amen.

Day 17—I Do Not Gossip

Men may talk about other people, but women know how to take it to the extreme. The first time I was hit with this realization, I was an adult. A group of women writers and I met online to help each other with our writing. The group was active and knowledgeable and I was tremendously grateful to be part of it; until one day when a disagreement came up about how the group should be run.

I didn't know what had transpired outside of emails to the group as a whole. I only know that the woman who had invited me into the group left gracefully but unexpectedly. The next day—without her presence—the gossip began. Horrible accusations flew through cyberspace about my friend. Unsettled but not sure what had happened, I bowed out of the group, saying simply that I was not comfortable in a group whose focus had moved away from writing.

That sounds godly of me doesn't it? But it wasn't. Because although I refused to contribute to gossip, I had made no attempt to find out the truth behind what was going on. After I spoke with my friend, I could clearly see that she had been wrongly accused.

I finally had both sides. But I had not stepped up to support my friend. I had not sought peaceful reconciliation. I had not done anything to stop the gossip from continuing. I had only removed myself from it.

Sometimes that is all we can do. Sometimes God calls us to do more—not to pompously or self-righteously stand above others and wag our fingers, but in humility to work for peace or point out the futility and pain of gossip.

Gossip is the spreading of rumors or lies about others or what other people have said. Theologians speculate on whether God ever actually told Eve not to eat from the tree of knowledge or whether Adam relayed the message to her. Scripture tells us clearly that God told Adam this.

> *And the LORD God commanded the man, "You are free to eat from any tree in the garden; but you must not eat from the tree of the knowledge of good and evil, for* ***when*** *you eat from it you will certainly die"* (Genesis 2: 16-18, emphasis added).

The New Living Translation says "if you eat from it, you will die." Philosophers and computer programmers refer to this as an *if/then construct.* A cause and effect. *If* you eat from it, *then* you will die.

But other Bible versions include a time element, like the New International Version above. *When* you eat; or *in the day* that you eat. Those versions do not have an if/then equation. There is an assumption that it will happen. *When it happens, you will die.*

This suggests that God knew Adam and Eve would eat the forbidden fruit. Of course He knew they would, because God knows all. Let's recap:

God told Adam not to eat from the tree of knowledge and then set about creating Eve. Whether God told Eve not to eat from the tree later is not recorded in Scripture. Obviously she knew she wasn't supposed to because she told the serpent so. But did you notice?

> *The woman said to the serpent, "We may eat fruit from the trees in the garden, but God did say, 'You must not eat fruit from the tree that is in the middle of the garden,* ***and you must not touch it****, or you will die'"* (Genesis 3:2-4, emphasis added).

Did Eve add "you must not touch it"? Did Adam add that when he relayed God's instructions to her? It is like the game of telegraph where the original message gets messed up the longer it travels between teller and receiver.

The serpent added further to the mix with his own "fact," that Eve would "be like God."

> *"You will not certainly die," the serpent said to the woman. "For God knows that when you eat from it your eyes will be opened, and you will be like God, knowing good and evil"* (Genesis 3:4-5).

Eve talked with Satan about God behind His back. She discussed with him what God had or had not actually said. She didn't go to God and ask Him to clarify His instructions. She didn't even just bow out gracefully and leave the presence of the serpent. Rather, Eve talked about God and either changed what He had said or believed what He might have said based on what she *wanted* Him to have said.

Satan proceeded to twist and change Eve's words (and God's) in a direction he wanted to take her. Satan began the gossip but Eve continued it and added to it. Satan showed us how gossip can destroy lives; how we must be wary of starting gossip, listening to it, spreading it or acting upon it.

If Eve were here she would say this was her story. She learned firsthand the danger of gossip. When the gossip with the serpent began, Eve should have stopped him right then or asked God for clarification. But she didn't. She pursued the thread of gossip to its fateful end.

Who are we to God? When we recognize the danger of gossip and refuse to be part of it, we understand how God might see His women of faith. We can answer:

I am like Eve.

For Thought and Discussion

- Can you think of a time when gossip hurt someone you cared about? How did it begin? How did it end?

- How do you react when someone starts to gossip? What might you do better to end the gossip before it gets out of hand?

- How can you pray for others without being involved in gossip as a side effect? ("We have to pray for her because, did you hear...?")

PRAYER: Heavenly Father, we're sorry when we participate in gossip. Please help us guard our tongues against that practice. Please help us focus only on what is true, noble and good for your kingdom. Amen.

Day 18—I Must Guard Against Seduction

Auctioneers can talk faster than my mind works. That's how I bought a silver tea service at about the price I would have paid anywhere else. Auctions are about getting caught up in the excitement of the moment.

Seduction is more subtle. Satan didn't yell at Eve or dance around her excitedly. He simply got Eve to question whether God had really said what she remembered Him saying. Then he appealed to her senses.

Our senses are a fabulous blessing. Hearing beautiful music, seeing glorious sunsets, smelling flowers, caressing a baby's downy head—all are wonderful blessings from the way God created our physical bodies. But hearing words we long to hear can make us believe what we want to believe instead of what we know is true. Seeing too much flesh can start our motors racing toward a sinful finish. The smell of alcohol can feed an addiction that dulls our spirits. Inappropriate touch becomes abuse.

> *Now the serpent was more crafty than any of the wild animals the LORD God had made. He said to the woman, "Did God really say, 'You must not eat from any tree in the garden'?"*
>
> *The woman said to the serpent, "We may eat fruit from the trees in the garden, but God did say, 'You must not eat fruit from the tree that is in the middle of the garden, and you must not touch it, or you will die.'"*
>
> *"You will not certainly die," the serpent said to the woman. "For God knows that when you eat from it your eyes will be opened, and you will be like God, knowing good and evil* (Genesis 3:3-5).

The very first thing Satan did was cause Eve to question what she knew.

> *"Did God really say, 'You must not eat from any tree in the garden'?"* (Genesis 3:1)

Satan was seductive by being vague. He didn't talk about the specific tree of knowledge at all. Satan first got Eve to question what God had said by quoting what he knew very well God had not said.

Let's break it down:

1. God told Adam and Eve they *could eat from any tree* in the Garden except the tree of knowledge. That's a positive statement. When Satan asked: Did God say you can't eat from *any tree*? Eve responded properly. No, God didn't say that at all. By forcing Eve to agree that God had *not* said that, Satan began the process of getting Eve to distrust what she remembered and also to question what God had actually said.

2. Then Eve added: You must not touch the tree or you will die. We don't know where Eve got the idea to add that statement. Maybe Adam added it to stress the importance of what God had said. Or Eve could have been trying to add to God's instruction in an attempt to argue with Satan.

If Eve was trying to argue with Satan, she learned an important lesson about arguing with the great Deceiver. Don't try. Instead, rely only on what God says. His Word is sufficient. And as Jude reminds us, we are to do what the archangel Michael did. Don't attempt to argue with Satan; simply ask Jesus to rebuke him (Jude 1:9).

3. Satan twisted God's words again, implying that God had said she would die either *from touching the tree* or *from eating the fruit* as if it was toxic or poison. God hadn't said she would die from eating the fruit. He had said that if she ate the fruit, she would die.

It wasn't the fruit that caused death. What caused Adam and Eve to die was God's judgment of no longer allowing Eve and Adam to eat from the tree of life. It wasn't *eating* a particular tree's fruit that caused death. Rather, it was *not eating* a particular tree's life-giving fruit that caused death. Satan spoke truth here. But he said it in a way that misled Eve. He seduced her. Deceived her. Twisted her thinking.

4. Then Satan appealed to Eve's desire to better herself. To have knowledge is a good thing. So Satan appealed to her brain and her common sense. That got Eve thinking. Who wouldn't want knowledge?

5. Eve also looked at the fruit. We can practically feel our mouths water as we think how lovely it must have been. All of

God's other food was great, Eve might have thought. This one must be fabulous. Like chocolate perhaps. Or lemon meringue.

There was one final step in Satan's seduction of Eve and he didn't even have to do or say a thing. Regardless of where Eve got the idea that touching the tree would cause her to die, when she actually picked the forbidden fruit from the tree, she touched it and didn't die. That must have felt like proof to her that all of Satan's other arguments were true, too. So she ate.

Satan first got Eve to question what she knew to be true. Then he got her to listen to arguments that sounded rational and for her benefit. And finally, he appealed to her senses. And those questions, rational arguments and sensory delights became the fall of mankind.

If Eve were here she would say this was her story. Eve learned that she must guard against seduction.

Who are we to God? When we learn how easy it is to be seduced, how subtle seduction can be; how rational it may sound as we fall into sin, but then seek to guard against it, we can learn the lesson Eve learned. When we do, we understand how God might see His women of faith. We can answer:

I am like Eve.

For Thoughts and Discussion

- Do you try to argue with Satan to justify your actions or immediately repent and turn to God?

- Can you think of a time in your life when you were seduced through subtle ways?

- How can we guard against subtle seduction in the future?

PRAYER: Heavenly Father, we sometimes lack clarity and wisdom and sometimes fail to see how the Evil One desires to seduce us and lead us into sin. Please guard our hearts and strengthen our minds against such seduction. Help us be strong in the face of evil. Amen.

Day 19—I Must Be Wary of Satan

When I was a kid, one Halloween, I wore red leotards and horns and thought I was being funny. In today's society, there is a sense that Satan is a myth. Although most people may grudgingly acknowledge the idea of a "higher power" or even God Himself, people outside of the church generally doubt the existence of Satan. They may believe there is evil, as done by bad people, but they decline to believe in a being referred to in Scripture as Satan.

Scripture tells us that the angel Lucifer—one of God's created beings—fell from grace and was cast out of heaven (Isaiah 14:12 KJV). As God does with so many characters in Scripture, He gave Lucifer a new name—Satan. Scripture also refers to Satan as the Evil One, the Devil, the Deceiver and the serpent in the Garden.

As Bible-believing Christians, we know that God is not just a mythical "higher power" or *Star Wars*-generated "force." God is real. And as Bible-believing Christians, we also know that Satan is real.

Eve had not heard of Satan. To Eve, the serpent was probably just another critter in the Garden. A talking critter, to be sure, but having no knowledge of good and evil until she ate the fruit, she had no way of knowing she should be wary of him.

We, however, have Eve's example. We also have Scripture to teach us about Satan's power and the results of listening to him. He slithers about our world, disguised and seeking to lure us away from God. We must be vigilant in looking out for him and steadfast in seeking protection from God.

> *Be alert and of sober mind. Your enemy the devil prowls around like a roaring lion looking for someone to devour* (1 Peter 5:8).

To make being vigilant in looking out for Satan even harder, Paul warns us that

> *Satan himself masquerades as an angel of light* (2 Corinthians 11:14).

Eve didn't know Satan before she ate the fruit. But she did after she had knowledge of good and evil. At that point she understood, saying, "The serpent deceived me, and I ate" (Genesis 3:13). She recognized her fault, but she also recognized who the Deceiver was because she could then recognize evil.

We have hope of protection from evil through Jesus, when God tells Satan:

> *And I will put enmity between you and the woman, and between your offspring and hers; he will crush your head and you will strike his heel"* (Genesis 3:14).

In other words, Satan's offspring (his demons) and Eve's offspring will be against each other. On first reading, we might think Eve's offspring means all of mankind. But the "he" who will crush Satan's head is singular. In other words, Eve's offspring refers to only one person. Jesus.

Jesus (having been born human through a human mother, Mary, also an offspring of Eve) will crush Satan with his heel (see also Romans 16:20 reminding us that God will crush Satan under His feet). Even God's punishment of Satan results in a blessing to us through Jesus.

If Eve were here she would say this was her story. She learned to be wary of Satan. She learned that Satan lies, seduces and twists truth to accomplish his desires.

Who are we to God? When we recognize that Satan is real and slithers about desiring us to sin and when we are vigilant in seeking protection from God, then we understand how God might see His women of faith. We can answer:

I am like Eve.

For Thought and Discussion

- Were you raised with the concept of Satan or was he a mythical figure to you? Has your view of Satan changed over the years as your faith has grown?

- How does God's promise that Jesus will crush Satan give you confidence in resisting evil?

- How might you view struggles with the seven "deadly sins" (anger, greed, pride, lust, envy, laziness and gluttony) as "discussions with Satan"?

PRAYER: Heavenly Father, thank you for promising us right at the beginning of mankind's existence that you will ultimately conquer evil. Thank you, Jesus for the promise that you will crush Satan for all time. Please help us be wary of Satan, Holy Spirit and call upon your power, Jesus to fight him for us. Amen.

I Grow in Understanding

Day 20—I Value Modesty

Last year, Jim and I headed to Cabo San Lucas and its glorious, sun-sparkled beaches. At one point, a bikini-clad woman walked by and Jim asked: "Isn't it interesting that women who generally wear modest clothing somehow don't have the same modesty when they hit the beach?"

It's considered appropriate to wear swimsuits at the beach but not to the grocery store. Yet, it's the same body; the same clothing; the same amount of skin uncovered.

> *Adam and his wife were both naked, and they felt no shame* (Genesis 2:25).

God created us without clothing. There's nothing bad; nothing evil about our bodies. They're beautiful—yes, even yours and mine. They function. They are miracles, performing properly (mostly) even when we aren't thinking about it or telling them what to do.

God doesn't make things that are inherently bad. In fact, after God made mankind, He declared it all "very good." So even if we stood out on the street corner naked, from a spiritual point of view, we should feel no shame about our bodies. The shame comes from Satan telling us we should feel shame.

Satan tells us we aren't good; we aren't perfect; our bodies are ugly or too fat or too lumpy, too shameful. And once evil came into the world, Satan found a way to use our bodies for evil. Part of woman's sense of protection from evil is to cover up her body so it does not encourage evil thoughts in others that might result in evil deeds. God recognizes that. Jesus said

> *But I tell you that anyone who looks at a woman lustfully has already committed adultery* (a sin) *with her in his heart* (Matthew 5:28, explanation added).

God created us without clothing. Our bodies themselves are not sinful or shameful. But once evil entered the world, even these glorious bodies could then be looked upon with lust and used for evil purposes. Therefore God fashioned clothing for us, right before Adam and Eve left the Garden.

> *The LORD God made garments of skin for Adam and his wife and clothed them* (Genesis 3:21).

God also instilled in women a sense of modesty. That sense of modesty is one of the characteristics God loves in His women. What constitutes modesty has changed over time from society's viewpoint. It might be impractical for us to go back to veils and floor-sweeping robes. But it is not impractical for us to stay within the confines of modern modesty. Paul tells us:

> *I also want the women to dress modestly, with decency and propriety* (1 Timothy 2:9).

Although our bodies are glorious in God's eyes, God's eyes are not filled with lust as man's eyes are. Modesty is for our protection from evil and also to help us maintain purity within our hearts and minds. Modesty is a gift from God straight to the heart of a woman.

I so love God's character. When God banished Adam and Eve from the Garden; banished them from the home they had known; banished them from the tree of life, resulting in physical death for all of us, before He let them go, God clothed them.

God recognized that Satan had brought evil into the world and caused Eve to know shame. So God covered her to protect her and reassure her that He could provide for all her needs—even her need to deal with shame over her body.

When we understand God's provision in this way, we recognize that even those very first clothes, designed and created by God Himself were a physical manifestation of how God was able to clothe mankind spiritually in His righteousness until Christ came Himself to complete the job. I like to imagine that those first articles of clothing, made possible from the first two innocent animals sacrificed to "cover sins" were the very first suits of the armor of God that Paul described (Ephesians 6:10-18), to protect Adam and Eve from the Evil One.

If Eve were here, she would say this was her story. Although God created her without shame, she understood the value of modesty, to protect herself from evil. She also recognized her need to be clothed in God's righteousness.

Who are we to God? When we recognize the value of modesty and of clothing ourselves in His righteousness, we understand how God might see His women of faith. We can answer:

I am like Eve.

For Thought and Discussion

- How do you feel about your body? Do you recognize its beauty? Do you feel shame over it?

- How do you think God sees your body? How might you begin to see it as He does?

- Are you modest? How modest are you compared to society's standards today? How can you encourage modesty in others?

PRAYER: Heavenly Father, we recognize that when you created our earthly bodies, you made us to be without shame. We're sorry when we feel shame over them. But thank you for giving us a sense of modesty and showing us how important that is to you. Please help us value modesty in ourselves and others. Amen.

Day 21—I Trust God's Word

I have to hear something three times from three different sources before I decide to believe it. Then when I do, I state it as if it's a fact I'd never heard before. That's when my husband blinks at me, wrinkles his dear forehead and says, "I told you the same thing last month and you didn't believe me."

Sigh.

I feel so much like Eve.

Eve also had trouble believing what she heard from those who loved her. Whether God told Eve directly not to eat from the tree of knowledge or whether Adam relayed that information to her, ultimately she didn't trust what they said—even though she knew they loved her and had her best interests at heart.

Yes, it was Satan who instilled that distrust into Eve. It was Satan who made her question what God had said. It was Satan who suggested God's motives themselves were bad. It was Satan who suggested that Eve—rather than God Almighty—might be on the higher ground, for her wanting to improve herself.

Eve loved God and wanted to be like Him. Therefore, to her mind, knowledge about good and evil was a good thing; eating the fruit was a good thing. As a result, Eve might have concluded that God's motives in keeping her ignorant must be bad. God didn't want her to be like Him; wanted to keep her under His control. She questioned His motives; she questioned the goodness of His rules; she questioned the goodness of God Himself.

Or if she had heard the rule—not from God—but from Adam, perhaps she questioned Adam's motives. Was he the one, rather than God, who meant to keep Eve in her place, ignorant of good and evil? Did she offer the fruit to Adam as a test to see what his true motives toward her were?

Although Scripture doesn't tell us the answer to those questions, the point is that Eve should have trusted those who loved her and distrusted what Satan told her. Similarly, we also should trust more what people who love us tell us than what we hear from strangers or from people in the world whose agenda does not coincide with God's. And above all, we should trust God's Word.

We saw on Day 17 that Satan and Eve misquoted what God had said, adding to His words or changing them entirely. Likewise we should be wary of doing so.

> *Every word of God is flawless; he is a shield to those who take refuge in him. Do not add to his words, or he will rebuke you and prove you a liar* (Proverbs 30:5-6).

Satan changed one word of God's command. God had said not to eat from *the* tree. Satan changed God's word to *any* tree. The danger and the lesson here from Eve about changing what God said is that changing even one word can lead us away from God's righteousness and toward Satan's agenda.

If Eve were here she would tell us she learned to trust those who loved her over Satan's lies. She would also say that she learned the danger of adding to or changing what God said.

Who are we to God? When we trust God and recognize the importance of not adding or removing anything from God's Word, we understand how God might see His women of faith. We can answer:

I am like Eve.

For Thought and Discussion

- Has God ever pointed out to you something in Scripture that you had previously misread and therefore misunderstood? What difference did it make in your understanding of God's character? What difference did it make in your faith?

- Have you ever added, removed or changed something in Scripture and discovered your error later? How did that make you feel? Or have you ever had to correct someone else? How did you do so? What was the result?

- Do you spend enough time with God's Word to know it?

PRAYER: Heavenly Father, sometimes in our enthusiasm for you we don't always get things right. Please remind us to focus strictly on what you tell us in Scripture. Please also reveal your truth to us so we can apply your Word to our lives. Amen.

Day 22—I Seek Knowledge

I'm the least educated member of my family. When I graduated from university, I felt guilty that I had no desire for a master's degree. But that didn't mean an end to my education. Continuing adult courses became the norm and within the Christian realm, I have not been absent from a formal Bible study in decades. Not because I'm so great at self-improvement, but because somewhere in my heart, God instilled in me the understanding that knowledge is a good thing.

God made us teachable and gave us minds to learn and grow intellectually and spiritually. He gave us curiosity and a desire to know even the unknowable.

> *When the woman saw that the fruit of the tree was good for food and pleasing to the eye, and also desirable for gaining wisdom, she took some and ate it* (Genesis 3:6).

Scripture tells us again and again that wisdom is precious. Although wisdom is not the same as knowledge, there is a connection. The more information we have; the deeper our knowledge, the better we are able to think, conclude, make decisions. The wiser we become.

> *Be very careful, then, how you live—not as unwise but as wise, making the most of every opportunity, because the days are evil. Therefore do not be foolish, but understand what the Lord's will is* (Ephesians 5:15-17).
>
> *Blessed are those who find wisdom, those who gain understanding* (Proverbs 3:13).
>
> *The heart of the discerning acquires knowledge, for the ears of the wise seek it out* (Proverbs 18:15).

Evidently Adam also desired wisdom and knowledge enough to eat the fruit when Eve gave it to him. Or possibly he was in deep need of wisdom and knowledge to the point that Eve specifically wanted him to eat and get smart! Either way, Eve was the first person in history to have desired knowledge enough to do something about it. Bad choice. But still, Scripture shows us that Eve desired knowledge.

God knows we have questions. We wonder about things. We seek answers. We desire understanding, wisdom and knowledge. And when we find understanding, wisdom and knowledge, sometimes we also find God. Right there. Where He has always been. Waiting for us to find Him.

God encourages our understanding and our desire for knowledge. Not everyone is meant to gain a PhD. Not everyone is even meant to attend school or learn to read. But Scripture tells us again and again, that having wisdom is precious and that wise people seek knowledge.

If Eve were here, she would say this was her story. She would recognize that God gave her a brain and a desire to learn and grow.

Who are we to God? When we recognize that God has made us want to seek knowledge, we understand how God might see His women of faith. We can answer:

I am like Eve.

For Thought and Discussion

- How do you value education? How does society value it?

- Do you have a desire to seek knowledge in a certain area of life; a vocation or hobby? How does that drive your passion for it?

- How do you use your education or knowledge to help others and build up God's kingdom? How might you do more?

PRAYER: Heavenly Father, thank you for giving us minds and hearts that desire to learn what you would have us know. Please nurture our minds to learn more about your world. Grow us into the women you desire and help us share our knowledge with others. Amen.

Day 23—I Seek to Know God

Christians sometimes debate over the difference between "head knowledge" and "heart knowledge" of God, especially when people who may know Scripture don't apply it or misquote it.

The Bible is God's Word; it is God breathed; useful for teaching and filled with God's promises. It shows us God's character and even explains part of His plan for the future of the universe. Knowing Scripture may only be "head knowledge" but it is important to have that knowledge because it encourages, enhances and enables the "heart knowledge" of knowing God and deepening our relationship with Him.

Eve didn't have an annotated Holy Bible with footnotes and commentary. She couldn't listen to radio preachers or watch altar calls on TV. But she did have a personal, one-on-one relationship with God Himself. Surely Eve loved God. She would have naturally desired to be like Him, just as we—knowing Jesus—seek to be Christ-like today.

> *"For God knows that when you eat from it your eyes will be opened, and you will be like God, knowing good and evil"* (Genesis 3:5).

It appealed to Eve that eating the forbidden fruit would help her be like God and maybe understand Him more fully. By taking action (eating the fruit) in order to "become like God," Eve displayed her childlike recognition that the most valuable form of knowledge is seeking to know what God is like.

Eve believed Satan's argument that knowledge of good and evil would make her like God. We may moan over her simplistic view, but don't we all desire to be godly women? If we were "like God" would we not understand Him more fully? Part of the problem with Eve's desire for knowledge about God was that she thought herself capable of being equal to God in the first place. The other part of the problem with Eve's desire to be godly was the way she went about doing it.

Eve tried to be godly by disobeying God.

Among the jewels in Scripture about wisdom and knowledge, one that relates directly to Eve's circumstance is Proverbs 1:7:

> *The fear of the LORD is the beginning of knowledge,*
> *but fools despise wisdom and instruction.*

It is good to seek wisdom, along with instruction. But the beginning of knowledge should always begin with obedience to God. We should look first to Jesus in all things. And we should look to Him with the reverence He deserves as the Lord of all.

The other part of seeking to be godly is that God alone has a proper vision of what God wants us to be. We cannot simply be imitators of characteristics we see in God. He is in the process of growing us into the women He wants us to be. As we seek to know

God, our part also includes seeking to allow God to have His way in our lives.

God placed in Eve's heart a desire for knowledge along with a desire to be godly. But she forgot to first look to the Lord with reverence in obedience when seeking that knowledge. If she had, perhaps God would have led her through her desire for that knowledge. Seeking knowledge about God is the best knowledge to seek. The key is to seek that knowledge from Him.

> *... let the one who boasts boast about this: that they have the understanding to know me, that I am the LORD* (Jeremiah 9:24).

In other words, Jeremiah reminds us that whatever boasting we do, the only boasting God recognizes as valuable is boasting that we know God and know that He alone is Lord.

When Jesus lived on earth among us, his life and teachings were recorded for us in Scripture. We seek to know God through Jesus' recorded life as well as through prayer and meditation. We seek to live like Jesus did. Eve wanted to be like God. What Eve didn't understand was that we should not desire *to be like God* but *to live* a godly life.

If Eve were here she would say this was her story. A desire for knowledge is good; but the best knowledge to seek is knowing God, seeking to live like Jesus did while on Earth, following His earthly example and learning it all from Him.

Who are we to God? When we recognize that God created us to seek knowledge about His character, His plan and how we fit into it, but keep Him first in all things, we understand how God might see His women of faith. We can answer:

I am like Eve.

For Thought and Discussion

- How much importance do you place on seeking knowledge about God's character? How might you nurture a desire to know God more?

- Often the best—and hardest—way to know God is to listen to Him, both by meditating on Scripture and being still in His presence. In what ways have you been able to do this? What are your challenges in doing so?

- How might understanding God's character better help you live more fully and with more power?

PRAYER: Heavenly Father, thank you for giving us Scripture and people in this world who can help us understand your character. Please use our knowledge to encourage our faith and deepen our relationship with you. Amen.

I Grow in Faith

Day 24—I Can Create Life

When my children were young, I felt like I hadn't slept in decades. "Never mind." I would laugh. "I'll sleep when they leave for college."

Then a friend whose kids were in college took hold of my shoulders, looked me in the eye and said, "No, that's when you'll never sleep again."

One morning, when I was a few minutes late visiting my 92-year old mother, she said she had been looking out the window, afraid a black and white police car would show up to tell her I had died in a traffic accident. We never stop worrying about the lives we bring into this world. Because the blessing of creating life comes with responsibility.

Eve became the first mother. After she gave birth to her son, Cain, she said:

> *"With the help of the LORD I have brought forth a man"* (Genesis 4:1).

What that first birth must have been like! Eve had no ob/gyn. There was no pediatrician on call. There was no birthing room, hospital, head nurse, anesthesiologist, midwife or breathing coach. Adam and Eve must not have had a clue. But God was there with Eve, giving her strength, helping her get through it all. God had already brought human life into the world twice before. He knew what He was doing even if Eve didn't.

Bringing forth a man was a miracle for Eve. Giving birth is still a miracle today. Every time. Every birth. And always with the help of the Lord. Whether we know it or not.

Eve first had two sons, Cain and Abel. Cain killed his brother and then moved away. Eve must have grieved three times—first for the death of her son, second for the way she had failed in mothering Cain that he had become a murderer and third for having lost the presence of both of her sons. But then God blessed Eve with another son—Seth.

> *"God has granted me another child in place of Abel, since Cain killed him"* (Genesis 4:25).

One child cannot replace another child in a mother's heart, but this verse recognizes Eve's pain and how a child helped her heal. This healing was made possible by her ability to create life.

The name Eve means *life*. Eve was able to create new life biologically. Obviously—except for Adam and Eve and baby Jesus—it also takes a man to create children. Not every woman has children; some by their personal choice; some by God's decision. Nevertheless God has given womankind the biological ability to bring children into the world.

In addition to the ability to create physical life, women also have the ability to create spiritual life; to raise up and nurture our own faith and that of the people God has placed in our lives. Not every woman has children of her own, nor has every woman had a mother who nurtured and protected her. That is an unfortunate reality of life. But the great part of that truth—the redemptive part of God at work in our lives—is that every woman can mother others, even if those people are not her own children.

When God created us in His image, He gave womankind an extra helping of His character trait of nurturing. He also gave us a heart for loving others, especially perhaps for loving the sweet hearts of children.

Is it a wonder that most children's writers are women? That most Sunday school teachers are women? That most school teachers are women? Women have a natural heart to nurture children. Even children who are not our own.

> *Jesus said, "Let the little children come to me, and do not hinder them, for the kingdom of heaven belongs to such as these"* (Matthew 19:14).

The most important legacy we can leave this world is that of a life well-lived for Jesus. The Gospel is a heavenly gift which Jesus expects us to spread to all corners of the world, starting first within our own homes. The Gospel can most easily be shared and passed down through our family and by the way we witness to our relatives and raise up our children.

> *"If anyone causes one of these little ones—those who believe in me—to stumble, it would be better for them to have a large millstone hung around their neck and to be drowned in the depths of the sea"* (Matthew 18:6).

A millstone is heavy. If we have one hanging around our necks, we will drown—even if the sea is filled with living water. That's how important this legacy is to Jesus.

As women we can give life—physically and by nurturing others. We can leave a legacy through our own children and by nurturing people who come into our life.

As God's children, our own spiritual lives also need nurturing. That means focusing on God, reading His teachings in Scripture, communicating with Him in prayer, attuning ourselves to the Spirit in us, opening our hearts to others. We can be nurturing to our own need to be mothered.

Eve was the first woman and became the first mother. Through her example recorded in Scripture, she can still mother and nurture us. We too can create and nurture spiritual life in others.

If Eve were here she would say this was her story. Eve was the physical mother to all mankind, following God's instruction to be "fruitful and fill the earth" (Genesis 2:28). So too, Jesus has commissioned us to go into the world and be fruitful, filling the world with His Gospel.

Who are we to God? When we recognize that we have the ability to give life to children as well as to nurture our own and others' spiritual lives, we understand how God might see His women of faith. We can answer:

I am like Eve.

For Thought and Discussion

- Have you experienced childbirth yourself or been with someone giving birth? Can you describe the pain, struggle, joy?

- Who nurtured you spiritually as a child? As an adult? Who in your life do you nurture? Who in your life needs nurturing?

- Do you spend adequate time nurturing yourself spiritually?

PRAYER: Heavenly Father, thank you for our lives and the lives of the people you've placed in our path. Thank you also for mothers and children and the ongoing line of faithful believers who love you. Thank you also for the women in our lives who have mothered us. Please show us who you would have us mother today. Amen.

Day 25—I Can Persuade Others

A little girl can wrap her daddy around her little finger so tightly it's like a tourniquet cutting off the blood supply to daddy's brain. Little girls can wrap their mommies around their fingers, too. My daughter excelled at that. I'm not sure how it worked with Daddy, but with me, it always included the word, "because."

I need a new…because.

We should do this…because.

You should say yes…because.

It all seemed so rational as it tripped off her wee little lips. Even at age three my baby girl had the power to persuade.

Did Eve have Adam wrapped around her little finger? We can assume that—with no other human around for company—Adam no doubt listened to what Eve had to say. She was clearly able to persuade him to do what she wanted him to do with the fruit. It doesn't sound like she even had to argue or try to make her point. She simply took some of the fruit and ate it.

> *She also gave some to her husband, who was with her, and he ate it* (Genesis 3:6).

Sometimes we persuade people by our words. Sometimes we persuade people by example, like Eve did. Since we have the power to persuade others, how much better to persuade them to follow Jesus? Beyond our ability to lead people to Jesus by our testimony, how we are living our lives? Are we a godly example of how to live like Christ? Or—like Eve—are we handing people the means to sin by what we do, how we treat others or how we live our own lives?

> *Let your conversation be always full of grace, seasoned with salt, so that you may know how to answer everyone* (Colossians 4:6).

Eve had the power to persuade Adam to do something bad. She didn't use her power to persuade Adam to stay away from Satan. She didn't try to get Adam not to succumb to temptation. And because Eve used her power to persuade in a bad way, both Adam and Eve fell into sin. We are marked by that sin to this day.

A blessing part of this calamity is that Eve's example of persuasion was recorded for us. Scripture recorded a tragic event that can teach us an important lesson. We have the power to persuade, by what we say, what we do and how we live.

Jesus commissioned us to introduce Him to others. We have the responsibility to share the Gospel; to share the truth of Jesus with the world. We have the responsibility to share our testimony—what Jesus has done for us personally—with others. We are to provide evidence, relate facts, share our story—and His.

Our job is not to make others believe. That is Jesus' job. Our job is merely to introduce people to Jesus and let Him take it from there. But our introduction is more powerful; more meaningful;

more impactful if it is accompanied by an example of a life well lived for God. Living by example could be the turning point; the persuasion of a lost soul, rescued for Him.

If Eve were here, she would say this was her story; she was aware of her power to persuade.

Who are we to God? When we recognize that we have the power to persuade; and when we then use that power to lead others to Christ, we understand how God might see His women of faith. We can answer:

I am like Eve.

For Thought and Discussion

- Have you ever introduced anyone to Christ? If you have, did you do so by arguing with words? How did your example of living affect your ability to persuade?

- How do you use your power of persuasion in your life with your husband; your family; friends; at work?

- Satan also used persuasion. Do you use his methods? Is there ever a place for that kind of persuasion?

PRAYER: Heavenly Father, thank you for giving us power to persuade others. Please teach us how to use this power more effectively to bring other people to you. And please teach us how to use this power more effectively to keep others from falling into sin. Amen.

Day 26—I Can Do All Things

We think of the record of Eve's life, as stopping at the Fall. But it was after she left the Garden that things got really hard. After leaving the Garden, Eve began having children. But there was no one to mentor her in being a mother. She had no on-duty nurse to call; no books on parenting; no neighbor woman who could give a helping hand. Everything Eve had to do she had to learn to do on her own. How to raise children. How to manage a home. How to meet the needs of the people she loved who depended on her.

Like modern mothers, Eve had trouble with her kids. Big trouble. She grieved for her murdered son and surely must have lived with guilt for how she had raised Cain. She was the first woman to deal with aging and face her own mortality. She was the first woman to have sinned. She was the first person who recognized she had disobeyed God. She must have dealt with depression and loneliness as she endured it all in her woman's heart.

The times have changed since those first days on earth. Nonetheless, Eve encountered many of the daily issues we still face today. We have others to teach us how to do things and help us when we can't do it all on our own. Eve had Adam. But more importantly, she also had the Lord. When Eve gave birth to her first child, she recognized she had not done so alone.

> *"With the help of the LORD I have brought forth a man"* (Genesis 4:1).

Paul reminds us that we can do all great things with the help of the Lord. We can do small things too. In fact,

> *For I can do everything through Christ, who gives me strength* (Philippians 4:13, NLT).

Giving birth is a really big thing. It was for Eve and it is for us today. But everything God desires for our lives is a big thing, if it is a "God thing." When we sense God asking us to do something big, most of us immediately feel inadequate to the task. When we go through a trial, we feel crushed or incapable of clawing our way out.

But God is always with us and the power of Christ—through the Holy Spirit living right here inside of us—strengthens us. We can do those really big things. We can do those really small things, too. Because we can do them through Christ who strengthens us.

With the help of the Lord.

If Eve were here she would say this was her story. No one had ever lived before she and Adam did. She faced crises, struggles, uncertainty, pain, guilt and loneliness. But she had God and because God was with her, she was able to live a big life.

Who are we to God? When we recognize that we can do all things with the help of the Lord, we understand how God might see His women of faith. We can answer:

I am like Eve.

For Thought and Discussion

- Has there ever been a time in your life when you felt isolated and incapable of doing what needed to be done? How have you used that experience to be more compassionate and helpful to others?

- Have you experienced the power of Jesus helping you do something you felt was beyond your personal ability? Describe the experience and the effect on your faith.

- Is there anything you sense God is asking you to do that you feel inadequate to accomplish? How might you use Eve's experience and rely on the Lord to push you forward?

PRAYER: Heavenly Father, thank you for teaching us that we are not alone in this great big world. When you remind us to take our small lives and make them big for your sake, please remind us also that you are with us, and that we can do whatever you ask us to do because you are doing it with and through us. Amen.

Day 27—I am Thankful for What I Have

I was really happy with mine until I saw hers. That one looks much better. I never get the good stuff. The grass is always greener on the other side of the fence.

God gave Adam and Eve the fruit from every tree in the Garden to eat, except one tree. He even gave them the fruit from the tree of life. Wow. Nothing could be better than that.

But it was the forbidden fruit Eve wanted. The one she was not allowed to eat. Eve looked at all of the fruit she had and compared it with what she didn't have.

She broke number ten of God's Ten Commandments: *Thou shalt not covet.* Obviously God hadn't given those Commandments to Moses yet. Maybe God should have had Adam chisel them out in gold and hang them next to the Pishon River. But God didn't. So maybe Eve didn't know she shouldn't covet the fruit. She *did* know she wasn't supposed to eat it.

But she wanted to.

Eve found herself feeling unsatisfied with God's blessings. God's blessings were for Eve's own good, especially His rule against eating the forbidden fruit. Still, the forbidden was tantalizing and Eve coveted it. Because she coveted it, she found His other blessings lacking. In Eve's mind, God's allowable food wasn't enough for her, she reasoned. She wanted more. She wanted what she thought would make her better, smarter, happier.

Remember, Eve looked at the forbidden fruit and saw that it was not only pleasing to the eye (looked delicious and appealed to her senses) but was also good for providing knowledge. Surely something both delicious and intelligent-making should not be withheld from her. If God *really* loved her, He'd want that for her, right?

We too think we know what we want and what is best for our lives. Often though what we want is contrary to what God desires for us. God's plan is always better than anything we could come up with on our own. God's blessings are always better than what we think we want to obtain on our own. But sometimes we get in God's way; doubt His way; conclude that God is holding back on giving us the good stuff that will make us better, smarter, happier.

Sometimes we simply want what we do not have. We covet what we do not have; those cool things others have. Their success. Their talents. Number ten of the Ten Commandments reminded us not to do this. So did Jesus when He said:

> *"Watch out! Be on your guard against all kinds of greed; life does not consist in an abundance of possessions"* (Luke 12:15).

Maybe possessions aren't the same as wanting a piece of fruit. But it is the same as wanting what is not ours. In fact, seen from this perspective, Eve also disobeyed Commandment number 8 when she stole what God had not given to her.

When we find fault with God's blessings or when we do not think His blessings are enough, we can be tempted into sin. Eve's sin encompassed not only disobeying God but also doubting His goodness. When immortal life was taken away from her, she recognized God's truth—not eating was way better than eating. God's rule had been good after all. His blessings were good. His provision was sufficient and faultless.

To put things into real-life perspective, do we eat more of God's perfect food or more of man's chemically-altered and preserved foodstuff? Do we feel somehow that God's food isn't enough? Are we finding fault with His provision? Do I really believe the candy bar I choose is better for me than the ripe strawberries God created?

Peter shared God's vision that all of God's food (meat) is acceptable. But, just as Paul cautioned believers not to test others' dietary restrictions, so must we determine where our physical needs fit with the dietary choices available today. As I write this, I recognize my own struggle over food that is not God's by design.

Modern food notwithstanding, Eve looked at all of God's provision available to her in the Garden and decided it was not enough. In essence, she doubted God's blessing. She wanted more than what God had graciously provided for her and Adam. Paul reminds us of a better way.

> *Do not be anxious about anything, but in every situation, by prayer and petition, with thanksgiving, present your requests to God. And the peace of God, which transcends all understanding, will guard your hearts and your minds in Christ Jesus* (Philippians 4:6).

Be thankful in all situations. Present your requests to God. If Eve had asked God about the fruit, He probably would have still said "no." Maybe He would have explained His reasoning to her.

Maybe not. But if Eve had focused on thanksgiving for God's blessings, she might have been able to overcome her dissatisfaction; might have been able to see how greater He had blessed her by not allowing her to eat the fruit.

What about our blessings? Are we satisfied with what God has given us or do we look at what others have and feel dissatisfied? When we bemoan our aches and pains, can we first be grateful we have bodies that mostly work? When we bemoan our jobs, can be first be grateful we have jobs or that we are able to work at all? How can we look at areas in our lives that we feel are lacking and see the blessings they contain?

Or if we cannot see blessings, can we thank God for being in charge and for knowing that He is with us through it all? Or can we thank God as He leads us to work with Him to change our circumstances and live a life more in line with the blessings He desires for us?

If Eve were here, she would say this was her story. She would have looked back on her life before she had eaten the forbidden fruit. She would have recognized that the forbidden fruit was not for her good. She might have recognized the importance of being thankful for what she had and might have trusted more in God's goodness.

Who are we to God? When we are thankful for God's perfect provision and trust in His goodness, we understand how God might see His women of faith. We can answer:

I am like Eve.

For thought and discussion

- Think of a time when you traded what you had for something you thought was better and discovered it didn't satisfy you. Describe your experience.

- How do you relate Eve's example of forbidden fruit to eating unhealthy food today? Do you struggle with foods you know are not God's desire for a healthy lifestyle? How do you reconcile this?

- What are you especially thankful for today that you may not have been thankful for yesterday? How can you change your perspective so you are more grateful—not necessarily *for* specific circumstances—but *in them*?

PRAYER: Heavenly Father, thank you for your blessings. Thank you for blessings we aren't even aware of that come from you for our own good. Help us be grateful and satisfied with what you provide. Amen.

Day 28—I am Eve

When I began writing this study, I started with annoyance at Eve's stupidity. I didn't want to write a book that suggested I might want to be like Eve or that (shudder) I might already be like her in my heart and soul.

But I determined to explore the subject and see what lessons Eve had to teach me. No sooner did I begin to look at her story through the lens of God's love and forgiveness than I began to extend grace to Eve and recognize God's grace extended to me. Very quickly into the writing of this study, I came to love my dear sister Eve. I now gratefully acknowledge that I have always been like her and—when I learn the lessons she struggled to learn herself—I want them to be part of my personal journey of faith.

Over the last 27 days, we have seen how Jesus made us in His own image, just as He made Eve. He formed us and breathed into us the breath of physical and spiritual life. He made us very good, giving us stewardship over the incomparable beauty of this earth and desiring us to be a helpmate and companion to others. Our challenge now is:

How does the realization of our place in God's world enhance our understanding of His love for us? How might it empower us to be a more active part of His world, living in it and sharing His love with others?

We have also seen that, just as God searched for Eve, God is looking for us. We realize that we can't hide from Him but are blessed to be able to seek Him and live in His presence. Our challenge now is:

How does this understanding encourage us to be more proactive in seeking to deepen our relationship with Him?

We have seen that, just as Eve had hardships, we must bear hardship, too. We sin, but are loved anyway and recognize that God's rules and His judgment are for our good. Our challenge now is:

How does this understanding of God's strength and ultimate goodness deepen our trust in His power in our lives?

We have seen, just as Eve did, that we can learn from our mistakes and must be wary of gossip, seduction, and Satan. Our challenge now is:

How does the fact that God made us teachable give us confidence in our ability to lean into God for His guidance and protection?

We have seen that, just as Eve should have first trusted God's Word, so should we. We value modesty and seek knowledge, especially understanding the heart of God. Our challenge now is:

> *How does this understanding help us seek to know God more fully and thus be better able to live the godly lives He desires us to live?*

We have seen that, like Eve, we can create physical and spiritual life. We can persuade others, rely on Christ for strength and be thankful in all circumstances. Our challenge now is:

> *How does this understanding help us move outward into the world to be Jesus' hands and feet, showing His love to others?*

Some of these lessons I have learned better than others. Some I still struggle with truly understanding. But I know that God is working in my heart and is loving me while He waits for the lessons to become a part of who I am.

And who I am is a one-of-a-kind woman of God; a woman loved by God and seen by God as He saw Eve and as He sees His other women of faith. This study is about Eve and her story. But it is also about every woman who loves God, who calls Him Father, calls Jesus brother and calls the Holy Spirit friend.

We may seek to live like Christ, but still we—as women—are very much like the first woman God created. Our lives are brand new and fresh in His eyes; just as brand new and fresh as that first woman. When we learn the lessons God desires us to learn from that first woman, we can say "I am like Eve."

Then perhaps God will smile and say, "It is very good."

Love, Eve

For Thought and Discussion

- What did you think about Eve at the beginning of this study? How has your perception or opinion of the story of Eve changed since you started this study?

- What lessons do you still struggle with learning?

- The name Eve means "life." How might this study help you live the meaning of Eve's name?

PRAYER: Heavenly Father, thank you for the lives of women recorded in Scripture. Thank you for their examples and the lessons we can learn from them. Help us live lives of love for you and for others because of the life we have in you, Jesus. Amen.

Studies in the

***With Faith Like Hers* series**

available or coming soon

I am Eve

I am Esther

I am Ruth

I am Mary (Jesus' mother)

I am Elizabeth

I am Rahab

I am Hannah

I am Deborah

Resources

Be sure to visit the author at www.CarolPetersonAuthor.com.

If you enjoyed this study, please let others know. One of the best ways to let folks know is to leave a review. Just go to Amazon.com, find the title of this book and click on "Write a Customer Review." Thanks in advance!

Sources

Biblegateway.com is a fabulous online resource. It provides a quick and easy way to read the same Scripture in various versions for deeper understanding. It also has quite good commentaries that encourage a desire to find out more.

Deen, Edith. *All of the Women of the Bible.* San Francisco: Harper San Francisco, 1983. [Interesting for a general overview of women in Scripture.]

Glo Interactive Bible. Immersion Digital, LLC, 2009. [Great resource for background and historical information about people and places in Scripture.]

Interpreter's Bible; The Holy Scriptures in the King James and Revised Standard Versions with General Articles and Introduction, Exegesis, Exposition for Each Book of the Bible. Volume III. New York: Abingdon Press, 1952. [This 12-volume Bible belonged to my Pastor dad who purchased them during or shortly after seminary. He used them for 45 years of sermon preparation. Now they're my first go-to when I need solid, theological commentary or explanation.]

OpenBible.info is another good online resource. I love the site's ability to search based on a word or topic. Although the results sometimes feel computer generated (because they are!) it's still a good place to start expanding a line of thinking.

Vine, W.E. *Vine's Complete Expository Dictionary of Old and New Testament Words.* Nashville: Thomas Nelson Publishers, 1996. [Helpful in understanding the meaning of the original words in Scripture.]

Zondervan NIV Study Bible. Grand Rapids: Zondervan, 2002. [Good, basic study notes for quick overview of Scripture.]

The best and most valuable source—always—is prayer, study and God's leading. It's easy and tempting to come up with personal theology and proclaim it brilliant. It's harder, but always best, to rely on God's leading and to check any "personal brilliance" against the truth of God's Word set forth in Scripture.

From the Author

I was raised in a Christian home—the daughter of a Protestant minister. But it wasn't until I was in my late twenties that I took full ownership of my faith and began the long process of learning what it means to be a Christian and a child of God. I'm still learning.

When I began writing for publication, I was blessed by early publishing success when my first four books were picked up by a respected educational publisher. My mission became to write in a way that would educate, inspire and entertain others.

Gradually I moved from writing for children to writing for young women and—more recently—to writing for women seeking to deepen their faith in Christ. Someone in the writing world once said that "all writing is basically autobiographical." That's true for me as I write this Bible study series. I seek to understand and deepen my own faith as I write to help other women understand and deepen theirs.

I live in California with my husband of more than 35 years. I have two grown children who taught me that if God only loves me a fraction of how much I love them—wow, God loves me a lot!

Made in the USA
Monee, IL
27 June 2021

71869504R00095